AF432369

The
Forever
Formula

Unveil the Eternal Laws
for Lifelong Achievement
And Timeless Success

The
Forever
Formula

Unveil the Eternal Laws
for Lifelong Achievement
And Timeless Success

Stephen R. Gorton

Copyright © 2024 by Green Stem Media.

All rights reserved. Except as permitted under the
United States Copyright Act of 1976, and in the case of
brief quotations embodied in critical articles and
reviews, no part of this publication may be copied,
reproduced or distributed in any form or by any means,
or stored in a database or retrieval system, without the
prior written authorization from the author.

First Edition published: 2024

www.greenstemmedia.com
South Jordan, Utah 84009

"For I know what I have planned for you, says the Lord, I have plans to prosper you, not to harm you. I have plans to give you a future filled with hope."

Jeremiah 29:11 (NET)

Table of Contents

Get More Out of This Book 13

Defining Success Differently 17

Divine Potentiality and Inheritance 51

Consecration and Sacrifice 83

The Virtue of Obedience 113

Love and Service 151

The Principle of Faith 191

Seek First the Kingdom of God 225

The Law of Probation 255

No Secrets 283

In a Nutshell 304

Success Quotes 311

About the Author 335

Get More Out of This Book

Sterling Sill, author of over 30 books, once wrote about an article he read entitled How to Get More Out of a Book Than There Is in It. "Good readers," he explained, "may be able to get out of a book all there is in the book, but with a little imagination and some ability to analyze, they may get much more." This potential for personal growth through effective reading and pondering is truly inspiring and should motivate us to delve deeper into our reading experiences.

All capable readers can have their thoughts strike a particular notion, causing their thinking to drift away from the material they read. We should not be too quick to return to the book. Instead, we should embrace the freedom of our imagination, allowing it to lead us to some interrelated way of thinking that could prove extremely valuable. This freedom of thought and imagination is liberating and opens our minds to new possibilities.

People may often find that the most significant insights, ideas, and beliefs are the ones that they come up with on their own, not so much from the concepts printed on the page. As our mind wanders along its own specific chain of correlated thought, we may arrive at some important interpretations and impressive conclusions all on our own. These personal insights and conclusions are empowering and should give us the confidence to trust our own intellect and understanding.

This is how to get more out of a book than there is in it. The book will cause us to come to conclusions regarding a diversity of notions not actually in the book. The interest of freeing our thoughts is a highly beneficial and rewarding undertaking.

Paul, the New Testament apostle, was a known ponderer. He advises us that "whatsoever things are true, whatsoever things are honest, whatsoever things are just, whatsoever things are pure, whatsoever things are lovely, whatsoever things are of good report… think on these things." [1] The ability to ponder gives us the capacity to obtain more from our circumstances and situations than what is actually in them. Through this procedure, we place ourselves above the conventional and commonplace existence.

Thousands of fantastic, fascinating philosophies are frittering away in countless books. Hundreds of essential and profound programs that could benefit us sit untouched on library shelves. Even the word of God Himself remains largely unfamiliar and unacquainted to many of us. All the essential ingredients for success in our personal pursuits can only advance our progression once we ingest and absorb them, once we get them circulating in our bloodstream, and make them a part of our inner strength and learning.

---

[1] Philippians 4:8.

As you read this book or any other, practice the art of pondering. It will give you a more prolific passion for learning and thinking and, hopefully, for putting into practice. If what you read here does not please and persuade you, so much the better. You can amend each step or chapter to fit your specific situation and satisfy your particular prerequisites.

Practical pondering will enable you to draw concrete conclusions and form compelling objectives on the vital subject of your progress and success in life. With this in mind, we have included a blank page at the end of each section titled Thoughts and Inspiration. This page lets you record your thoughts, ideas, insight, or inspiration. Don't just copy the author's words; write down your thoughts and get more out of this book than there is in it.

Introduction:

Defining Success Differently

"O how I love thy law! It is my meditation all the day.
Thou through thy commandments hast made me wiser than mine enemies:
For they are ever with me.
I have more understanding than all my teachers:
For thy testimonies are my meditation.
I understand more than the ancients, because I keep thy precepts.
I have refrained my feet from every evil way, that I might keep thy word.
I have not departed from thy judgments: for thou hast taught me.
How sweet are thy words unto my taste! Yea, sweeter than honey to my mouth!
Through thy precepts I get understanding: therefore I hate every false way."

Psalm 119:97-104

Success is a deeply personal journey, uniquely defined and measured by each individual. For one, it may be the thrill of achieving a long-held dream, while for another, it could be the satisfaction of overcoming a personal challenge. Each of us holds the power to shape our own path to success.

Success is a multifaceted concept, encompassing a myriad of definitions. It can be the discovery and nurturing of our unique talents, the joy of contributing to others in meaningful ways, or the fulfillment of personal and professional goals. This diversity of success invites us to explore and define our own unique paths to achievement.

At its core, success is about achieving personal goals, big or small, that bring us fulfillment and joy. It's not about meeting external expectations, but about finding our own paths to happiness and satisfaction. This understanding of success encourages us to prioritize our own well-being and happiness in our pursuit of achievement.

Thousands of books have been written on the subject of success. Many of these works approach success primarily from a worldly or "temporal" point of view. They often focus on wealth creation, offering strategies for financial growth and investment.

Another common theme is material abundance, teaching readers how to accumulate possessions and enjoy a lifestyle filled with luxuries. Career enhancement is also a frequent topic, providing advice on climbing the corporate ladder or building a thriving business.

However, this perspective can be limiting. True success encompasses more than just tangible rewards. It involves personal fulfillment, mental well-being, and meaningful relationships. We need a more holistic sense of success that enriches all aspects of our lives.

People often equate success with earthly possessions and money. These are sometimes the natural by-products of a grander goal. Material wealth can seem like an indicator of one's success. However, this isn't necessarily true in all cases. Many who possess great wealth may still lack fulfillment and happiness. Material success is undeniably valuable and worth striving for. Achieving financial stability and career milestones brings a sense of accomplishment and security. However, it has its limitations.

Accumulating wealth or status is only one facet of a fulfilling life. Emotional well-being, strong relationships, personal growth, and meaningful societal contributions are equally important. Material achievements alone cannot provide lasting happiness or a sense of purpose. Success can be measured in terms of health and well-being. Living a balanced, stress-free life might indicate a successful life despite a modest income.

The definition of success is deeply personal and varies from person to person.

Total success encompasses more than just tangible rewards; it's about balanced growth in all areas of life. While wealth and material goods can indicate certain types of achievement, they aren't the sole markers of a successful life. True success encompasses much more than just financial stability or luxury items. It's about finding joy and purpose in your journey.

We must decide for ourselves what success means to us. Personal success is personal. It is whatever we want it to be that is worthy of us as children of our Father in heaven. Components of our overall success should include:

• Good health and the physical energy to enjoy our success;

• Meaningful relationships (someone to share our success with);

• A love of life and living (which is something that money cannot buy);

• Mental stability and awareness;

- and, of course, peace of mind.

There is nothing mysterious about success. Success is the power to realize an objective and obtain an anticipated outcome. Success is the aftermath of correct behavior. Material rewards and spiritual blessings result simply from following successful formulas. Apart from its material or spiritual rewards, success should be viewed as a tremendous ability to achieve.

Success literature has evolved in recent years, encompassing broader perspectives beyond material wealth. These works delve into deeper dimensions of success that transcend superficial materialism. Many of these teachings draw inspiration from Eastern philosophies and religions.

Unlike traditional approaches focused solely on financial gain, these new teachings promote finding balance and harmony in one's life. Personal fulfillment and inner peace are prioritized alongside worldly achievements. This balanced approach encourages a more meaningful and enriched life. This literature appeals to those seeking comprehensive success by merging practical goals with elevated ideals. It offers a path where prosperity coexists with profound personal growth.

In recent years, there has been an increase in success literature that considers the subject on a broader, somewhat higher level than mere materialism. Success teachings based on Eastern philosophies and religions approach the subject of success from a more elevated plane than simple materialism or wealth creation. However, they include and support worldly success.

However, most of the concepts in these books are like stones skipped on a pond. They touch the surface of truth here and there but never sink into the pure depths of what our Father in heaven has revealed to us. These ideas may glimmer briefly, creating ripples that capture our attention momentarily. Yet, true wisdom lies far deeper. Divine insights demand more than just a cursory glance.

Today, we need a more spiritual approach to the laws that govern successful living. Surface-level understanding won't suffice in navigating life's complexities. By grounding ourselves in eternal truths, we connect with enduring principles that withstand shifts and trends. This deeper approach offers not only guidance but can transform our very being. It aligns us with the Divine will and provides clarity amid chaos.

In his famous book, *The Seven Habits of Highly Effective People,* Stephen R. Covey writes, "There are principles that govern human effectiveness—natural laws in the human dimension that are just as real, just as unchanging and unarguably 'there' as laws such as gravity are in the physical dimension." Anytime a specific success technique works, it works because its principles are parallel to and consistent with eternal laws and principles that govern human effectiveness.

People who "produce" effective programs for human development and achievement are merely putting the eternal concepts of success into modern terminology, making them more acceptable and enticing to a new age. John Taylor stated, "We talk about the great discoveries men have made connected with electricity, steam, light and its properties, and a variety of other principles that exist in nature; all these principles are governed by certain specific laws, which are immutable and unchangeable; *and all of the great discoveries which men have made, have only developed certain properties that have always existed.* They have not invented anything." [2]

True success becomes attainable only when rooted in divine principles. All the principles and formulas employed to achieve success in our lives can be traced to and have their roots in the eternal gospel of Jesus Christ. Whenever we learn a principle or a law that brings us a successful outcome, that law is based on true gospel principles. When we discover a natural law of the universe, a "new" secret to success and human development, we

---

2 Taylor, John, *Journal of Discourses* 16:371.

also find that unchangeable and undeviating eternal principles govern it.

"These are principles," stated Wilford Woodruff, "that you cannot annihilate. They are principles that no combination of men can destroy. They are principles that can never die…. Not one jot or tittle of these principles can ever be destroyed. I would to God the world could understand this." [3] Our "discovery" is actually something that God has placed here and that has always existed.

Wilford Woodruff also teaches us that "there is a law given unto all kingdoms, and all things are governed by law throughout the whole universe. Whatever law anyone keeps, he is preserved by that law, and he receives whatever reward that law guarantees unto him. It is the will of God that all his children should obey the highest law." [4]

We can find the formula for every success in life within the gospel of Jesus Christ.

---

[3] Woodruff, Wilford, *Journal of Discourses* 22:342.
[4] Woodruff, Wilford, *Millennial Star* 48:801.

There is an intrigue in accepting and practicing the mysterious. The timeless teachings of Tibet, ancient instructions from India, and spiritual guidance from gurus all have a particular mystical attraction. The oriental philosopher teaching us to awaken the solar plexus, the Indian sage advising us to visualize the object of our desire, and the contemporary scientist imploring us to impress the subconscious mind are all, in their own terminology, expounding the principle of "as thou hast believed, so be it done unto thee." [5]

All truth is eternal. It remains constant and unchanging even if the language in which it is stated changes. Truth is still truth, whether articulated in the eloquent phrases of the ancient apostles or the precise scientific jargon of our contemporary age. Despite changes in method and language, the essence of what is expressed transcends time, culture, and methodology. Unique phraseologies, modern language or expressions, original interpretations, or varying emphasis are not

---

[5] Matthew 8:13.

necessarily indicators of a departure from truth. They are, to the contrary, evidence that the truth is being comprehended with new familiarity to human desires and needs and is becoming more universally understood and accepted. Truth must be taught to each generation and every people in new and different terms. [6]

Therefore, objectively analyzed, the Savior's statement to the centurion, "As thou hast believed, so be it...," contains the same truth as modern science's explanation that the law of attraction correlates thought with its object. The only difference is in how it is presented to us.

In religious terms, faith and belief are seen as divine principles that can manifest desired results. On the other hand, modern science explains this phenomenon through psychological and energetic principles, suggesting that positive thoughts attract corresponding realities. While one approach is rooted in spiritual doctrine, highlighting a

---

[6] See D&C 1:24.

connection with a higher power, the other relies on empirical evidence and scientific theories.

The gospel teaches us that success is harmony with true principles. It is obedience to correct, fundamental laws. "The abundant life," wrote Paul Dunn, "can best be achieved through the practical application of true gospel principles." Simply put, success is the discovery of truth and the achievement of harmony with that truth.

This is the more spiritual approach to success.

- # -

Thoughts & Inspiration

We all strive to succeed in life. Our ambitions drive us to reach new heights and create fulfilling futures. Success is not just about wealth but also finding happiness and contentment. We seek the good things in life—comfort, health, and meaningful relationships. These elements enrich our lives beyond material gains. True success encompasses personal growth and the joy of experiences, each new experience adding a unique color to our journey. For many, achieving high success means realizing their fullest potential.

To achieve this desire, we must first recognize that there are two different forms of success: real success and false success. Real success aligns with our core values and principles, consistently reflecting the true essence of what we aim to accomplish.

On the other hand, false success may appear impressive on the surface but lacks a meaningful foundation. It often stems from goals that do not resonate with our genuine desires and ethical standards. For instance, a person who climbs the corporate ladder at the expense of their personal relationships or health may be achieving a form of false success.

If our objectives stray from these fundamental laws and values, achieving such goals amounts to nothing more than false success. This type of accomplishment is hollow and unfulfilling in the long run.

For instance, approximately every two minutes, someone in the United States attempts suicide. Each day, nearly seventy people succeed—but is that true success?

True fulfillment comes from pursuing endeavors that genuinely matter to us and uphold our integrity. By aligning our ambitions with our deeper purpose, we ensure that our successes are authentic and satisfying, and our journey is filled with purpose and meaning.

Given that life is everlasting, our earthly, temporal accomplishments have significance only as they affect our eternal success. The Forever Formula, a set of principles based on the revealed word of God, examines the achievement of success in this life and in the life to come. These principles, which include material success, career success, wealth creation, self-improvement, true happiness, and the like, are designed to guide us toward a more eternal and enduring form of success.

In his audio program, *Lead the Field*, Earl Nightingale defines success as the "progressive realization of a worthy goal." By this definition, we are successful whenever we are on course toward fulfilling a worthy goal. Success, then, lies not solely in achieving the goal but in the journey toward the goal, a journey that is filled with learning, growth, and opportunities. When we are working toward the things we want to accomplish, we are successful.

"We are at our best," wrote Mr. Nightingale, "and we are happiest, when we are fully engaged in work we enjoy on the journey toward the goal we've established for ourselves." This is perhaps what Cervantes meant when he wrote: "The road is better than the inn."

Author and Physician Deepak Chopra defines success as "the continued expansion of happiness and the progressive realization of worthy goals." The prophet Joseph Smith declared that: "Happiness is the object and design of our existence; and will be the end thereof, *if we pursue the path that leads to it.*" [7]

True success and happiness go hand in hand. As Carl Trumbull Hayden explains, the difference between the two is that "success is getting what you want, and happiness is wanting what you get."

One of the names given to the gospel of Jesus Christ is The Great Plan of Happiness. This plan outlines principles and values that, when followed, invariably lead to a life of

---

[7] Smith, Joseph, *History of the Church* 5:134, 135.

happiness and fulfillment. When we follow the true principles of Christ's gospel, we are invariably led down a road to happiness. Whenever we find truly happy people, we will find they are living some principle of the Great Plan of Happiness.

"Peace of mind," wrote Stephen R. Covey, "comes when your life is in harmony with true principles and values, and in no other way."

- # -

Thoughts & Inspiration

Earl Nightingale relates the humorous story of a minister walking by a beautiful farm. The minister noticed that the fields were well cultivated and abundant with crops. The fences were freshly whitewashed and in good repair. The house, barn, and yard were clean and well-kept. The minister noticed a farmer working in the fields and called out to him, "God has certainly blessed you with a beautiful farm."

The hard-working farmer looks up, thinking momentarily, and then answers, "Yes, He has, but you should have seen it when He had the place all to Himself."

Each of us has been given our own "farm" to tend to—our life and calling in this world. We can choose to build successfully on what may seem at times to be the unimpressive plot of earth we inherit, or we may decide to allow it to fall into disarray with no real direction, purpose, or objective. Whichever we choose, the farm is still the same. What we do with our inheritance is what makes the difference. The potential for growth, abundance, and success is always there, waiting for us to recognize it. We must realize that our success and fulfillment as children of God depend upon our response to the eternal truths we have been given.

The people in Old Testament times learned that when they fall away from God, the natural laws of the universe become their enemy. In Enoch's time, when the people became extremely wicked, "the earth trembled, and the mountains fled… and the rivers of water were turned out of their courses; and the roar of lions was heard out of the wilderness."[8]

This apparent hostility in nature is because plants, animals, and minerals abide by

---

the established laws of their Creator. The entire universe and everything in it comply with the specific edicts of their design. We are the exception. Only human beings, the offspring of God, refuse to obey even the most sensible and self-exalting principles.

In a conference address given in October 1970, Richard L. Evans stated: "The seasons, the sunshine, the growing seeds; heat and cold; the life of a child; the harvest we have—these are not theory, and the same authority that runs the universe on such precision also gave us commandments to keep, commandments that are still in force… *the spiritual and moral laws are as much in force as are the physical laws, and each person is going to be what he lives*… Each one will realize the results of what he does and thinks—the results of how he lives his life." [9]

The only real power we humans have is the ability to adapt ourselves to the

---

[9] Evans, Richard L., Conference Report, Oct. 1976. pp. 87, 88.

eternal laws for lifelong achievement and timeless success.

The Lord wants to help us advance from one success to the next until He can move us to where He wants us to be. His goal for our success is: "Be ye therefore perfect, even as your Father which is in heaven is perfect." [10] Our ability to accept this goal for ourselves will indicate the degree of success we will achieve.

The eternal laws for lifelong achievement and timeless success relate to our temporal success. Still, they are as everlasting as any law given by God for the benefit of His children. Our success in this life or the next depends on aligning ourselves with these principles. This alignment provides us with a sense of direction and guidance, reassuring us that we are on the right path.

Law exists in all things and all places.

---

[10] Matthew 5:48.

"And unto every kingdom is given a law, and unto every law there are certain bounds also and conditions.

"All beings who abide not in those conditions are not justified." [11]

For God to remain God, He must obey every law in existence, completely and totally, in all His kingdoms. To achieve true and lasting success, we must abide by the rules and principles revealed to us for this kingdom.

"There is one thing of which I am absolutely certain," wrote Sterling W. Sill, "and that is the one business of our lives is to succeed. God did not go to all the trouble of making this wonderful earth with its great natural laws and then expect us to waste our lives in failure. He did not create us in His own image and then endow us with potentially magnificent minds and the godly powers of personality and spirit *without having in mind a divine destiny for us on the highest level...* The

---

greatest waste in the world is that human beings, you and I, live so far below the level of our possibilities. Compared with what we might be, we are just partly alive." [12]

Orson Pratt further explains: "But another and still greater object the Lord had in view in sending us down from yonder world is this, that we might be redeemed in due time, by keeping the celestial law, and have our tabernacles restored to us in all the beauty of immortality. Then will we be able to multiply and extend forth our posterity and the increase of our dominion without end." [13]

Jesus exhibited a life lived under perfect control. He had absolute knowledge of good and evil but never once found it advantageous or desirable to deviate from His purpose. He did not need to turn to the right or left to know its disadvantages. The godly nature of Jesus Christ is the ultimate expression

---

[12] Sill, Sterling W., *That Ye Might Have Life*, p. 22.
[13] Pratt, Orson, *Journal of Discourses* 14:242.

of success. It is the purest and most authentic form of success.

Thoughts & Inspiration

Divine Potentiality and Inheritance

"What does man in reality know about God and of his laws; or the proper fitness of things? What does he know about that vitality that he himself is in possession of?"

John Taylor (JD 21:342)

"Ye are Gods."

Psalm 82:6

The idea of divine potentiality and inheritance is the first Forever Formula for Success. This concept is founded on the truth that we are literally spiritual offspring of our eternal Father. Our higher spiritual nature is that of children, children of a loving Deity who has promised us all that He has. Our natural state is one of divine potential and infinite inheritance, a state that empowers us and inspires us to reach our highest potential.

In an address given in 1884, George Q. Cannon stated that "it is a glorious truth that has been taught to us, that we are literally the children of God, that we are his [*sic*] literal descendants, as Jesus was literally descended from Him and that He is our father as much as our earthly parent is our father, and we can go to Him with a feeling of nearness, knowing this, understanding it by the revelations which God has given us." [14] What greater success can we hope to achieve than to become like God? What more tremendous wealth could be ours than to be heirs of God and joint heirs with Jesus Christ? This divine inheritance, this shared ownership with the Creator, is a testament to our worth and significance.

Realizing our true spiritual nature and understanding and appreciating our divine potential allows us to achieve any dream we have. Our possibilities, being eternal and unlimited, are not bound by the constraints of the physical world. The expression and experience of our spiritual self, or self-referral, as it is often called in today's terminology, teaches us that our internal reference point is our spirit, not the physical, worldly environment surrounding us. "But there is a spirit in man: and the inspiration of the

---

[14] Cannon, George Q., *Journal of Discourses* 25:155.

Almighty giveth them understanding." [15] Without that spirit, what are we?

Engage in this simple yet profound experiment. Stand before a full-length mirror and gaze at your reflection. What do you perceive? Ask yourself, "Am I the physical body that stands before me, or am I the consciousness that perceives this body?" This question, though seemingly unanswerable, is a crucial step in our spiritual journey. Many of us shy away from it, but to truly enrich our lives, we must embark on the path of self-discovery.

Losing any part of the physical body does not diminish you as a person. For instance, if you were to lose an arm, you would not say, "I am nothing without my arm." If you were missing a leg, you would not say, "Without that leg, I am nobody." You are not just your body. Nor are you just your mind. You are something much more significant. You are spirit. Your spirit is the entity that uses your body as a vehicle and your mind for its

---

[15] Job 32:8.

personal expression. Your spirit is the entity that makes the choices that create your life and your world. The real you is the spiritual entity within. Even though the body may be complete with all its parts, it is lifeless, motionless, and inanimate without the spirit.

When we are burdened with misconceptions about our true spiritual nature, our faith is clouded. We become mere particles in motion, seemingly filled with knowledge we only pretend to possess. Without a clear understanding of our spiritual nature, we are lost. We do not know whom to call, whom to pray to, or whom to turn to in times of need. The truth is that we only know what God communicates to us and can understand only what He allows and reveals. Understanding our spiritual nature is the key to enlightenment and inspiration.

"And this is life eternal," explained Jesus, "that they might know thee the only true God, and Jesus Christ, whom thou hast sent." [16] To know, comprehend, and understand the

---

[16] John 17:3.

Being who created us, who gave us eternal life, *is* life eternal. When we fully understand this concept, we approach God with increased confidence. We ask God for that which we desire as easily and as confidently as we ask our earthly father.

"For in him we live, and move, and have our being; as certain of your own poets have said, For we are also his offspring." [17]

"We are the offspring of that Being," remarked Brigham Young in 1869, "each and every one of us, no matter who we are. If we go to the West, East, North or South or to the uttermost parts of the earth, and gather up the human family and bring them here, they are the offspring of that Being whom we worship as God." [18]

The Gospel of the Kingdom of God brings us into a special relationship with God. The everlasting Gospel, through the atonement of Jesus Christ, brings us into a

---

[17] Acts 17:28.
[18] Young, Brigham, *Journal of Discourses* 12:324.

closer relationship with God, our Father, and makes us heirs to all the promises that God has made to His children. God is truly our Father, and we are literally His children.

"For as many as are led by the spirit of God, *they are the sons of God.*

"For ye have not received the spirit of bondage again to fear: but ye have received the spirit of adoption, whereby we cry, Abba, Father.

"The spirit itself beareth witness with our spirit, that *we are the children of God*:

"And if children, then heirs: heirs of God, and joint-heirs with Christ; if so be that we suffer with him, that we may be also glorified together." [19]

Every species of being begets its own kind. When mature and grown up, the offspring become like the parent. The offspring of God, our eternal Parent, are

---

[19] Romans 8:14-17.

endowed with the potential to grow up and become literally gods or sons of God.

Orson Pratt stated, "We are the sons and daughters of God just as much so as the children, present this afternoon, are the sons and daughters of their parents, and in the same light, that we are the children of our earthly parents so are the children of men the offspring of the almighty. He is our Father in the full sense of the word, and we were begotten by him, and born to him, not in this probation, but in the world prior to the existence of this one—in our former or first estate. There we were born, there we were begotten, there we received a spiritual existence in the image of God." [20]

"You have got to learn to be gods yourselves," stated Joseph Smith, "and to be kings and priests to God." [21]

---

[20] Pratt, Orson, *Journal of Discourses* 19:281.
[21] Smith, Joseph, *Discourses of the Prophet Joseph Smith*, pp. 40,41.

"Jesus answered them, Is it not written in your law, I said, Ye are Gods?" [22]

When we accept our true spiritual nature and allow it to fulfill its purpose without opposing it or offending it (because this would disable its influence on us), it will re-create us in Jesus Christ, making our flesh, blood, and bones anew, creating the entire person anew. We are then born from above and sanctified unto God.

"I do not pretend to understand the secret springs that are subject to the Almighty's touch," remarked Orson Hyde, "but suffice it to say that I know they exist, and that He can touch them aright; and if we will sense them and honor Him and keep His commandments, *He will touch them every time in our favor.*" [23]

The objective and foremost purpose of our life, and the entire basis of our existence, is to become better children of our Father in

---

[22] John 10:34.
[23] Hyde, Orson, *Journal of Discourses* 11:153.

heaven. We are children of God working toward a divine destiny.

Without a clear understanding of our spiritual nature, our internal reference point becomes our selfish ego. The ego, however, is not who we are. It is only our self-image, a social mask that characterizes the role we choose to play in life.

As we begin to recognize our true relationship with God, we are empowered to co-create our own successes, our own consequences, and our own outcomes. This realization is not just a shift in perspective, but a transformative power that brings hope and empowerment.

Success is created by harmony, and it is through an understanding and acceptance of who we are and what we may choose to do that brings us the success we experience in every aspect of our lives.

Eastern philosophies call this karma. In science, it is known as cause and effect. The scriptures refer to it as reaping what you sow.

Whatever terminology we apply, it is the same
eternal principle.

- # -

Thoughts & Inspiration

By aligning our will with God's will, we unleash a powerful force within us. We become the cause, and we create the effect. We sow the seeds of our future. Our creative power, the key to our success, lies in our thought process. We have the ability to discipline our minds to think only those thoughts that manifest the effects we desire in our lives.

How can we apply the law of divine potentiality and inheritance to our daily earthly existence?

If we want to enjoy the benefits of divine potentiality and fully utilize the creativity that is inherent in us as children of God, we must know how to access and use that creativity. The affluence of the universe, the extravagant array of abundance on this planet, is an expression of God's creative mind. The more "tuned in" we are to God's mind, the more we will have access to His infinite, unbounded creativity.

The Creator constantly emits creative thoughts and fills an ever-expanding universe for His creations to develop into. As children of God, we are able to participate in this ongoing process of creation.

Ask yourself these questions: Have I attached a purpose to my thoughts, or do I allow them to flow in random streams of consciousness? Are the thoughts running through my mind constructive and purposeful, or are they just replays of old programming?

Listen carefully to what is going on in your mind!

If you are like most people, most of your thoughts consist of negative input or useless chatter. However, we must think thoughts that contribute to our eternal happiness and success.

In his book, *As a Man Thinketh*, James Allen writes: "Until thought is linked with purpose there is no intelligent accomplishment. With the majority, the bark of thought is allowed to 'drift' upon the ocean of life....

"They who have no central purpose in life fall an easy prey to petty worries, fears, troubles, and self-pitying's, all of which are indications of weakness, which lead, just as surely as deliberately planned sins (though by a different route), to failure, unhappiness, and loss, for weakness cannot persist in a power-evolving universe."

The most outstanding ability we possess is the power to think. However, only some of us know how to think constructively; consequently, we achieve only indifferent results. We should always examine our thoughts, intentions, and desires as the ultimate cause of our experiences in life.

"Of all the beautiful truths pertaining to the soul which have been restored and brought to light in this age," continues James

Allen, "none is more gladdening or fruitful of divine promise and confidence than this—that man is the master of thought, the molder of character, and the maker and shaper of condition, environment, and destiny.

"As a being of Power, Intelligence, and Love, and the lord of his own thoughts, man holds the key to every situation, and contains within himself that transforming and regenerative agency by which he may make himself what he wills."

If our lives and world are not as perfect as we would like them to be, then we must simply change our thoughts.

Thoughts & Inspiration

One of the most effective ways to access the creative powers of the Father is through the daily practice of prayer and meditation. This requires committing to a certain amount of time and concentrating on communicating with Deity. It requires periodically withdrawing from such activities as watching television, listening to the radio, playing video games, social media, chatting online, or (yes, I'm going to say it) even reading. It demands that we set aside a little time every once in a while to draw closer to our Father in heaven, to open and keep open the lines of communication with Him.

The universe is governed by law, and there must be a cause for every effect. The same cause, under the same conditions, will invariably produce the same outcome.

Consequently, if prayer has ever been answered, it will always be answered if the proper conditions are complied with. This must necessarily be true; otherwise, the universe would be in a state of chaos instead of perfectly and precisely controlled, and God would cease to be God. The answer to prayer is subject to law, and this law is definite, exact, and scientific, just as are the laws governing gravity and electricity.

It may be difficult for some of us to exercise faith in an unseen being or to believe that God can communicate with us, that He hears and answers our prayers, that He is our Father, and that He loves us. Our increasing technology, miraculous medical achievements, plentiful wealth, and comforts have caused some of us to ignore the need for continual prayer to our Father. We echo the statement from Job's time, "...what profit should we have if we pray unto him?" [24]

We should realize the transformative power of prayer as we seek success in building

---

[24] Job 21:15.

our lives. It's true that "except the Lord build the house, they labor in vain that build it." [25] Prayer is a real, and vital force in life, and if we want to increase our success, we must learn to make our prayers effective, knowing that they have the power to transform our lives, instilling hope and inspiration in our hearts.

Prayers can ascend beyond this world to our Father in heaven, in word as well as in thought, and He has the power to answer them. To the worldly, prayer is a psychological crutch. To the true believer, it is the avenue of communication with our unseen Father. To the unbelieving and rebellious, it is an act of senseless piety. To those who have tasted its fruits, it is the secret to achieving our greatest aspirations.

The type of prayer established by God is not vain repetitions, insincere lispings, or memorized rhetoric. It is a prayer based on knowledge, nurtured by faith, and offered in spirit and in truth. Such prayer opens the door to success and happiness in this life and eternal

---

[25] Psalm 127:1.

life in the world to come. Unless and until we make prayer a daily part of our existence where we regularly address our Father and, by the power of His Spirit, listen to His answers, we are not yet living a truly successful life. The scriptures teach us: "In everything by prayer and supplication with thanksgiving let your requests be made known unto God." [26]

Effective prayer is when we know we are heard, and our prayers will be answered. We must believe that we are praying to a God who hears and answers prayers and who is interested in us and our success. Modern literature refers to this concept as tuning our minds' vibrations and frequencies in with the universal mind's vibrations and frequencies. In Gospel terms, we call it "inspiration."

How many of us realize the incredible power of prayer? Do we truly appreciate what an enormous blessing it is to call on our Father in heaven, knowing that he is interested in us and wants us to succeed? God is not a

---

[26] Philippians 4:6.

prosecuting attorney trying to convict us for our sins. He is not trying to discount us for every error we make. He is not some cosmic competitor trying to show us up. He is a loving Father who seeks our success and eternal happiness and will help us achieve all we can if we give Him the opportunity to do so.

Effective prayer does not consist of words alone. Our prayers must be a perfect blend of feeling and spirit. The spirit teaches us to pray. It makes our heartfelt desires conveyable and acceptable. When a contrite spirit and a humble heart are united with faith, our prayers become significant, no matter how simple the words.

Prayer is more than mere introspection, contemplation, and quiet reflection. It is more than lifting ourselves by our bootstraps. Inarguably, by taking time to pause and reflect, we become more conscious of certain dispositions or inclinations and, through such self-awareness, are better prepared to master our weaknesses and control our frailties. And there is definite merit in such activity. We should pause occasionally and evaluate ourselves to determine our strengths and weaknesses, set goals for improvement, and plan ways to reach those goals. But such reflection, even with bowed head and bent knees, cannot correctly be called prayer.

Prayer is more than mere contemplation of one's life. It is a personal communion with Deity, a sacred moment that brings our attitude and spirit in harmony with the Divine. It is a direct and intimate communication between man and God, and between God and man. We do not merely commune with a world spirit, a universal mind or an ethereal or imaginary being. We communicate with a real being, God the eternal Father. Prayer is an interchange of thoughts and ideas. We express our thoughts to God and frequently experience or feel thoughts and inspiration in return, a sign of His love and care for us.

Prayer is a powerful force in the universe and in our personal lives. It bears fruit in direct proportion to the seriousness with which it is undertaken and according to the faith and diligence of the person who prays.

All success requires effort and answers to our prayers come only through effort. Anything worth having will cost us a part of our physical being, a part of our intellectual power, and a part of our spiritual strength. The advice we have been given is: "Ask, and it shall be given you; seek, and ye shall find; knock, and it shall be opened unto you." [27] But we have to ask, we have to seek, we have to knock. This emphasis on effort in prayer should motivate us and instill a sense of determination in us, knowing that our efforts in prayer will not be in vain.

"When we get home to our Father and God," wrote Brigham Young, "will we not wish to be in that family? *Will it not be our highest ambition and desire to be reckoned as the sons of the living God, as the daughters of the Almighty, with a right to the household, and the faith that belongs to the household, heirs of the Father, His wealth, His power,*

---

[27] Matthew 7:7.

His excellency, His knowledge, His wisdom? Ought it not be our highest ambition to attain this?" [28]

---

[28] Young, Brigham, Journal of Discourses 11:326.

Thoughts & Inspiration

DIVINE POTENTIALITY AND INHERITANCE

3 STEPS FOR PUTTING FORMULA

NUMBER ONE INTO EFFECT

I will put the first Forever Formula for Success into effect in my personal life by making a commitment to take the following steps:

1. As a child of God, I will develop my relationship with my Father in heaven by actively listening to the voice of His Spirit.

2. I will control my mental attitude and practice thinking positive, uplifting, and pure thoughts. I will keep my thoughts focused on the conditions I wish to create in my life and not allow them to wander in aimless streams of semi-consciousness.

3. I will find the time and make the effort to pray effectively for at least 15 minutes each day.

Consecration and Sacrifice

"There can be no progress, no achievement without sacrifice."

James Allen

"It has been generally understood among us that the redemption of Zion would not occur upon any other principle than upon that of the law of consecration."

George A. Smith (JD 17:59, 60)

The second Forever Formula for Success is based on the principles of consecration and sacrifice, also called giving and receiving. Although the words consecration and sacrifice may convey more of a sentiment of giving, millions of people worldwide can testify that when they have given freely, they have received abundantly.

Success experts emphasize the importance of giving back to the universe, of creating or contributing to a flow or exchange of energy. Money, a tangible form of this energy, plays a crucial role. Some experts even advise us to tithe a portion of our income to keep the universe's abundance circulating in our lives. By giving up ten percent, they explain, the subconscious mind is taught that there is more than enough. But even the law of tithing, though ordained of God, is a lesser law.

In the 44th Annual Conference of the Church, Orson Pratt declared that we are the most blessed people on the face of the earth. "God has gathered you from among the nations," he declared, "you were the only people to whom the message of life and salvation was sent... You harkened unto those missionaries and the counsels of God… Hence, you have done better than all other people, and you have been blessed above all other people." [29]

There is a real danger, as we become partakers of the Spirit and receive increased blessings and gifts from God according to our faith, that we will become proud and arrogant because we have received an abundance of the wealth of this world. This is the cycle that was repeated so often among the Nephites. We may feel we are a little better than the poor people who labor incessantly in menial tasks

---

[29] Pratt, Orson, *Journal of Discourses* 17:31.

for mere survival. But this is different from what Orson Pratt meant. Any one of us who feels he is better than or distinguishes himself from the poorer people of this world, supposing that he belongs to a higher class of society, is in danger of the same pride that destroyed the Nephite population.

To counter this danger, God has established a higher order in regard to property, guiding us in the responsible management of our material wealth.

Generally speaking, pride arises out of a love of riches. Material wealth and earthly possessions are the gods of this world; they are sought after more eagerly than any other object or condition by the people of the world and are quite literally worshipped by them. Their hearts are set on their earthly belongings.

The key to achieving success in earthly possessions and wealth is to understand that the earth and everything in it belong to the Lord. We are not owners, but stewards over His possessions, accountable for how we use and manage them. As Brigham Young pointed out: "Through our faith, patience, and industry, we have made us good, comfortable homes here, and there are many who are tolerably well off, and if they were in many parts of the world, they would be called wealthy. But it is not ours, *and all we have to do is try and find out what the Lord wants us to do with what we have in our possession, and then go and do it.* If we step beyond this, or to the right or to the left, we step into an illegitimate train of business. Our legitimate business is to do what the Lord wants us to do with that which he bestows upon us, whether it is to give all, one-tenth, or the surplus." [30]

Orson Pratt stated that the law relating to the full consecration of our property would perhaps be one of the last laws fulfilled before Christ's second coming.

"If we have the privilege of consecrating all we have," he wrote, "let us do it freely, and voluntarily, and that will be pleasing in the sight of God, trusting in Him who holds the heavens and the earth in His

---

[30] Young, Brigham, *Journal of Discourses* 16:10.

own hands, who holds the creations of eternity in His own hands, and sways His scepter over kingdoms and worlds without number, and controls them according to His will and pleasure… If we would do His will, and seek the riches that is the will of the Father to bestow upon us, we should be the richest of all people; for the riches of eternity should be given to us." [31]

If we were to honestly seek the riches that are God's to give for the sole purpose of heaven, we would be the richest people on the planet. The riches of the earth are God's to give, and He would freely give them to us. He could easily turn the riches of the earth into our hands if we were only prepared to receive them and use them according to his will. God knows the secret intents of our hearts. He knows whether we are prepared to use these riches to build His Kingdom or if we harbor selfish purposes.

---

[31] Pratt, Orson, *Journal of Discourses* 2:265.

John Taylor made the following statement regarding earthly possessions: "Mankind everywhere and in all ages have universally manifested a desire to obtain the things of this world—gold, silver, houses, lands, possessions, etc. This desire is inherent in man, it was planted in our bosoms by the Almighty, *and is as correct as any other principle* if we can only understand it, control it, and rightly appreciate the possessions and blessings we enjoy." [32]

---

[32] Taylor, John, *Journal of Discourses* 15:267,268.

Thoughts & Inspiration

The word of God reveals that the earth is the Lord's and the fullness thereof. [33]   Since the earth is the Lord's, along with the fullness of it, it does not belong to you or me. If the Lord had set apart and consecrated a particular portion of the earth to us through some deed or covenant, then we might claim it as our own. However, specific laws exist pertaining to this earth and the wealth the Lord has placed on it. In March 1831, the Lord stated, "it is not given that one man should possess that which is above another, wherefore the world lieth in sin." [34]

Orson Pratt explains that this is an element of the more perfect law and an indicator of the order of things God intended

---

[33] Psalm 24:1.
[34] D&C 49:20.

us to live by. As long as there is inequality in the things that belong to the Lord—the earth and the fullness thereof—the world lies in sin. We were never intended to possess more than another.

So then, why do some scrimp to save pennies in a jar while others own oil wells? How can one person possess millions of dollars while another struggles to make ends meet, and yet both are equal? They actually both possess the same, not as their own, but as stewards of the Lord's property.

If we are not equal in earthly things, we cannot be equal in heavenly things. There must be equality in worldly things so that we may be equal in heavenly things. If we were to divide the world's riches evenly so everyone has an equal share, everyone would have more than two million dollars, but in less than twenty-four hours, there would be inequality again. One person would soon possess more than another. This is the only way it could be: changes, difficulties, and lack of good judgment in the management and control of property, all of which would soon combine to make the divided shares unequal. Someone would lose a large portion of property through mismanagement; another perhaps by fire, by thieves, or in some other way. If all the wealth were equally distributed among all the people of the world today, tomorrow we would, through circumstances beyond our control, again be unequal.

However, equality can be established based on eternal principles that can never be destroyed. Inequality in earthly possessions would not exist, and nothing could happen that would make us unequal. When we accept these principles, we will be equal in wealth and earthly property, which will prepare us to be equal in heavenly matters, as well.

The Lord has required that everyone in His kingdom lay all things, not just one-tenth, but *all things* before the Bishop of the church. We are commanded to consecrate everything we own. We are admonished not to keep back even a portion, like Ananias and his wife, but to give everything and wholly consecrate everything we own.

The principle of the law of consecration initiated the settlements of Jackson County, Missouri. The revelations given and acted on at that time indicate that the members were to bring their property before the Bishop and consecrate it. Consecrated lands were purchased, and "inheritances" or stewardships were distributed among the Latter-day Saints, who regarded the property as property of the Lord.

Certain Saints, however, did not obey this law of consecration. They were more interested in looking after themselves than building God's kingdom. Believing they would soon become a great city, they purchased large tracts of land with the intention of later selling them to increase their personal wealth.

Is it any wonder that the Lord suffered the enemies of Zion to rise against them?

Imagine for a moment what could have happened if the people had obeyed this law, in every respect, when it was first given. Instead of the inequality between individuals in the church today, we may have had a completely different order of things. Still, their hearts had too much covetousness for a full consecration.

Orson Pratt explains that the key to consecrating property is remembering in the first place that what we have is not ours. When we consecrate what we habitually call our own, we are, in reality, only returning to the Lord what is His all along. We may possess something according to our earthly laws but not according to the laws of God. Unless God has directly given us what we claim to own, we do not own it according to the great principle and order God has established by celestial law. We may have earned it through labor, trade, and skill, but it is still the Lord's. When we consecrate our property—it all goes into the hands of the church. If all the church members were to consecrate in this way, they would have nothing left of their own.

If we were to consecrate everything in our possession, we would have perfect equality before we are awarded our stewardship. As far as property is concerned, we would be in a state of equality, owning nothing. The Lord would then say: "Let the Bishop appoint to everyone a stewardship." The Bishop, who has the authority to manage and control the Lord's property, would award each of us a specific stewardship. If anyone received double the stewardship, it would still not be his. He merely has stewardship of what belongs to the Lord. Consequently, he is still perfectly equal with his neighbor.

Since all property belongs to the Lord, and since we are His, we shall inherit it with Him, and it shall all be ours. If everyone possesses the whole, as joint heirs with the Lord, we still have equality. We become possessors of the whole, inheriting all things. We are joint heirs with Christ in the inheritance of the earth and of the fullness thereof. As Orson Pratt stated: "It is not a *division* of property that is going to bring about a oneness among the Latter-day Saints in temporal things, but it is a *union* of property." [35]

God never intended that everyone should possess an equal amount of stewardship. He has endowed some of us with a more remarkable ability to manage and control property than others. As in the parable, He gives to one person one talent, to another five, and to another ten, to make use of according to His instructions and to be accountable to Him. "It is required of the Lord, at the hand of every steward, to render an account of his stewardship, both in time and in eternity." [36] If we undertake to squander our stewardship, God will take it away, and give it to another, wiser steward who will manage His property so as to benefit the entire Church. [37]

When we give an account of our stewardship according to the laws and principles which the Lord has ordained if we have been wise and faithful, God will then say:

---

[35] Pratt, Orson, *Journal of Discourses* 2:100.
[36] D&C 72:3.
[37] See Matthew 25:14-30.

"Well done, good and faithful steward; thou hast been faithful over a few things, I will make thee ruler over many things." [38] One indication of our success is God's willingness to enlarge our stewardship.

Temporal things are a type of heavenly things. All things have their likeness, both temporal and spiritual. [39] The consecration of our earthly possessions is typical of a celestial order. We are all anxious to enter into a fullness of celestial glory, to inherit thrones and dominions, principalities and powers, to have kingdoms appointed to us, and to receive crowns of glory. To get there, we must begin where we are now to learn the eternal laws of success that exist there. Suppose we continue to have a division of property here and never practice the consecration of earthly goods as God has ordained in His law when we inherit our kingdoms. In that case, we will not understand how to manage those kingdoms properly. We might remember having read

---

[38] Matthew 25:23.
[39] See D&C 77:2.

something about it or heard it mentioned once or twice in Sacrament meetings, but we need practical application to know how to manage our celestial glory or the kingdoms and worlds placed under our charge. Since we are accountable, not only in time but in eternity, for our stewardship, we should try to live the order of things here, which is typical of the order hereafter.

Brigham Young has stated: "If we could perceive and fully understand that all the ability and knowledge we have, every good we possess, every bright idea, every pure affection, and every good vision of mind from our infancy to the present time, are all the free gift of the Lord, and that we of ourselves have nothing original, we should be much better prepared and far more ready to act faithfully and wisely under all circumstances. Every good thing is in His hands, is subject to His power, belongs to Him, and is only handed over to us, for the time being, to see what use we will make of it." [40]

Success is a matter of living that is not confined to the boundaries of this life. This life is merely a rehearsal for our eternal life ahead. God has a fortune to share with His children, and we may take as large a portion as we desire through the appropriate and faithful management of our temporal stewardships.

If we improve, demonstrating that we can be diligent and faithful in all the blessings bestowed upon us, then the principle of increase will be ours.

- # -

---

[40] Young, Brigham, *Journal of Discourses* 2:300.

Thoughts & Inspiration

There is no such thing as a sacrifice; it is a misnomer. King Benjamin taught his people that "all that [God] requires of you is to keep his commandments; and he has promised you that if ye would keep his commandments ye should prosper in the land; and he never doth vary from that which he hath said; therefore, if ye do keep his commandments he doth bless you and prosper you.

"And now, in the first place, he hath created you, and granted unto you your lives, for which ye are indebted unto him.

"And secondly, he doth require that ye should do as he hath commanded you; for which if ye do, he doth immediately bless you; and therefore he hath paid you. And ye are still indebted unto him, and are, and will be, forever and ever; therefore, of what have ye to boast?" [41]

Would you call it a sacrifice to invest some of your income in Microsoft, Apple, or Xerox and then receive a handsome return on it? What we do in the kingdom of God is the best investment we can make. It pays back the most even though we cannot fully understand it, for "eye hath not seen, nor ear heard" [42] the dividend that will accrue to the faithful in this Church and kingdom. There is virtually no sacrifice about it. It is like investing a portion of your income in time, to gain eternal riches, and such a sacrifice sinks into insignificance in a second. The greatest sacrifice we could make, even of life itself, is as nothing to those who are faithful.

Our earthly property should not be dearer to us than our salvation. It should be used to build up the kingdom of God. Heber C. Kimball stated, "When we… turn in our property, it will become empowered with the

---

[41] Mosiah 2:22-24.
[42] I Corinthians 2:9.

attributes of God and His Son Jesus Christ and the Holy Ghost, and all those who act with them in the eternal worlds, and from them to us, and from us back to the throne of God." [43]

"This principle of submission, and being controlled in property matters, is a doctrine which belongs to the Gospel and the building up of the Kingdom of God," stated Lorenzo Snow. [44]

This law is to continue as long as salvation continues. It has never been replaced. The law of tithing did not replace it. The law of tithing is a lower law and does not forbid us from obeying the higher law, the eternal law of celestial union in earthly things.

As true disciples of Christ, we have received a call not only to forsake the pursuit of worldly goods for personal gain but also to follow the commandments and build God's kingdom on earth. We do this by using the goods God has given us to use in His Church,

---

[43] Kimball, Heber C., *Journal of Discourses* 4:249.
[44] Snow, Lorenzo, *Journal of Discourses* 16:274.

and by forsaking the allure of worldly possessions for personal profit.

Thoughts & Inspiration

CONSECRATION AND SACRIFICE

3 STEPS FOR PUTTING FORMULA NUMBER TWO INTO EFFECT

I will practice consecration and sacrifice in my personal life by committing to take the following steps:

1. I will unselfishly give something to everyone I meet, even if it is only a smile, a compliment, a prayer, a positive thought, or a desire. As long as I am giving, I will be receiving.

2. I will be open to receiving. I will, with gratitude, receive all the gifts life has to offer me in whatever form they may come.

3. I will commit all that I am and all that I have, my wealth, my property, my time, and my talents, to building God's kingdom on earth.

The Virtue of Obedience

"For every action there is an equal and opposite reaction."

Sir Isaac Newton

"To obey is better than sacrifice."

1 Samuel 15:22

Jesus relates the parable of a man who went out to sow. His seeds were good, but some fell on stony ground, and others fell among the thorns. The seeds sown on stony ground grew rapidly, but the sun's powerful rays caused them to dwindle and die. The cares of the world choked the seeds that fell among the thorns. Some of the seeds fell on good ground, took root firmly, and produced a hundred-fold of ripe, delicious fruit.[45]

Jesus presented these ideas to show the people how they might fail and the danger of receiving God's word without having good and honest hearts. Paul teaches that we "see through a glass, darkly." [46] One of the reasons for

---

[45] See Mark 4:3-20.
[46] 1 Corinthians 13:12.

this is that our eyes are not fully opened by obedience to God's word.

Obedience, the third Forever Formula for Success, is a beacon of hope. It is often referred to as the first law of heaven and is also known as the law of cause and effect. It is the promise of reaping what you sow. No other virtue can compensate for obedience. It is the path to a hundredfold of ripe, delicious fruit.

Obedience has almost lost popularity among the "if it feels good, do it" crowd. Modern society seems to think it has the privilege of doing whatever it pleases. The truth is we only have the privilege of doing what is right. "There is not an iota in the revelations," stated Brigham Young, "from Adam down to the present day, but what requires strict obedience." [47]

All success is predicated upon law. The Lord revealed through the Prophet Joseph Smith that: "There is a law, irrevocably decreed in heaven before the foundations of this world,

---

[47] Young, Brigham, *Journal of Discourses* 13:92, 93.

upon which all blessings are predicated—And when we obtain any blessing from God, it is by obedience to that law upon which it is predicated." [48]

By implication, we may assume that not only is there a loss of blessings but also definite handicaps and disadvantages from disobedience to law. The Lord said: The Lord said: "I am bound when ye do what I say; but when ye do not what I say, ye have no promise." [49] Obedience or disobedience to law is the basis of all success (blessings) and failure (the loss of blessings). The consequences of disobedience are not to be taken lightly.

Obedience toward God is righteousness toward God. If we love God, we will keep His words. [50] To achieve true success in this life, we must obey every word that proceeds from the mouth of God. [51] This is our

---

[48] D&C 130:20,21.
[49] D&C 82:10.
[50] See John 14:15.
[51] D&C 84:44.

guiding light, our reassurance in the journey of life.

If we find it challenging to obey the celestial laws that God has revealed to prepare us to enter His presence, we should at least follow a lesser law. By obeying the lesser law, we will receive the blessings associated with that law. This concept of 'lesser law' is a compassionate provision from God, allowing us to progress step by step towards greater obedience.

We are at cause. If we harmonize our thoughts with spiritual law, we will be enriched.

The Doctrine and Covenants makes the following premise: "Whosoever is faithful unto obtaining these two priesthoods of which I have spoken, and the magnifying their calling, are sanctified by the spirit unto the renewing of their bodies... All that my Father hath shall be given unto him... Therefore all those who receive the priesthood, receive this oath and covenant of my Father, which he cannot break, neither can it be moved." [52]

Speaking of these verses, Wilford Woodruff asks: "Do we comprehend these things? Do we comprehend that if we abide the laws of the priesthood we shall become heirs of God and joint-heirs with Jesus Christ?" [53]

The most profitable idea in the world is obedience to God. No one has ever gone wrong following divine direction. It is easy to do right when we are sure of the answers, but Jesus indicated a higher kind of accomplishment when he said to Thomas: "Because thou hast seen me, thou hast believed; blessed are they that have not seen, and yet have believed." [54] And why shouldn't we believe? As Ralph Waldo Emerson said: "All that we have seen teaches us to trust God for all that we have not seen."

---

[52] D&C 84:33-44.
[53] Woodruff, Wilford, *Discourses of Wilford Woodruff,* p. 80.
[54] John 20:29.

The apostle Paul said: "All things work together for good to them that love God." [55] If we love God, think right, have the right attitudes, and do the right things, then everything will turn out in our best interests. "And hereby we do know that we love him, if we keep his commandments." [56]

- # -

---

[55] Romans 8:28.
[56] 1 John 2:3.

Thoughts & Inspiration

Obedience to eternal law, a concept deeply rooted in philosophical and spiritual traditions, means aligning our actions with the fundamental truths that govern the universe. Living in accordance with these principles leads to inner peace and a sense of harmony with the world around us. This path of obedience transcends mere external compliance and resonates at the core of our being, nurturing a profound understanding and respect for the world around us.

Though it sounds simple and easy, it requires balancing life and gaining maturity, perspective, and insight. Law is practical. It rewards us in whatever way we use it. If we use it to build up, it builds us. If we use it to destroy or tear down, it tears us down. Again, we reap precisely what we sow.

It's not that we don't know the way, but rather our inability to stay on track, that creates such a hindrance. Shakespeare said: "I can easier teach twenty men what were good to be done, than to be one of the twenty to follow mine own teaching."

We would make considerable progress toward ultimate success if we could learn to follow the best direction available. Staying focused on these optimal pathways often requires discipline, critical thinking, and sometimes the courage to embrace unconventional solutions. By continuously evaluating our actions and their outcomes, we can refine our strategies and better align them with our long-term goals. The journey may be challenging, but each step forward builds momentum toward achieving a more profound sense of accomplishment and fulfillment.

The rewards for obeying eternal law are beyond imagination. "But as it is written, Eye hath not seen, nor ear heard, neither have entered into the heart of man, the things which

God has prepared for them that love him." [57] Brigham Young taught us that "the blessings and bounties of the Lord upon us are bestowed according to our faithfulness and obedience to the requirements made of us… But to secure His blessings the Lord requires the strict obedience of His people. This is our duty." [58]

Obedience to law means being in harmony with law. We may then use the principles of that law to better our lives and make them more effective. By being in harmony with the laws of aerodynamics, we have learned to fly. By understanding and using the principles of optics, we can now view incredible distances into the heavens or gaze at an infinitely tiny world through a microscope. By obeying the laws of electronics, we speak and are seen and heard on the other side of the world.

Science is a textbook of natural law. Being in harmony with those laws has allowed the marvels of modern science to manifest

---

[57] 1 Corinthians 2:9.
[58] Young, Brigham, *Journal of Discourses* 12:99, 100.

themselves in our world. Spiritual laws, like the laws of the physical world, are clear and precise. When we obey these laws, we are granted rewards and advances, just as when we obey physical laws. Ignoring or defying spiritual law is just as unquestionably harmful. But by understanding and obeying these laws, we can navigate our spiritual journey with confidence and reassurance.

Laws, either physical or spiritual, are indications of the great forces and truths of the universe. Every natural law affecting man's fabulous flights into space had to be kept in the minutest detail. The laws of physics, the law of gravity, the laws of chemistry, and every law related to flying had to be understood and applied by the flight engineers. These natural laws were not seen as restrictions or impediments to successful flight but as the means for successful flying. Flight engineers must apply all the laws on which their success depends.

The same is true for being successful in life. To be an accomplished musician, a world-class athlete, earn a college degree, and achieve anything of value in life, we must set our goals and then determine which laws, properly obeyed, will make it possible for us to succeed. If we continually fight or refuse to obey the laws, we will become frustrated, begin to rebel and fail to accomplish our desires. But by understanding the laws that govern success and diligently obeying them, we can feel empowered and in control of our destiny.

We mentioned that obedience is also the law of cause and effect, of reaping what you sow. It means taking a particular course of action and accepting the consequence of that action. Every action produces a force of energy that is similarly restored to us. Sir Isaac Newton taught us that every effect results from a cause. The impact of our actions will, in turn, become a cause. This cause will bring about other effects, which will produce additional causes. When we put the law of obedience into action, we start a train of endless possibilities for good.

What we sow is what we reap. If we sow good, we shall reap good. "The problems in life," wrote Stephen R. Covey, "come when we are sowing one thing and expecting to reap something entirely different." To create happiness in our lives, we must sow the seeds of happiness; to create success, we must sow the seeds of success.

"If we never sow gloomy, despondent, or evil principles, we shall not be likely to reap them," commented Orson Hyde in a conference address given in 1859. "If we sow cheerful, lively, and good principles, we shall most likely reap an abundant harvest of the same; for, according to that which a man soweth, that also shall he reap. Let us learn to restrain every evil feeling; for if we give them birth, there is no telling the amount of evil they may create, and when or where they will end their work of death." [59]

- # -

---

[59] Hyde, Orson, *Journal of Discourses* 7:314.

Thoughts & Inspiration

We live in a world of multiple choices. God requires that we have every possible freedom to prove ourselves. In every moment of every day, we have access to infinite choices. We can choose how we react to situations, who we spend our time with, what thoughts we entertain in our minds, and which goals we prioritize. Each decision shapes the trajectory of our lives in ways both small and large. The power lies within us to create a life that aligns with our deepest values and aspirations.

By becoming more aware of the choices available to us, we empower ourselves to live more intentionally. This means not merely drifting through life reacting passively to external events but actively shaping our own path. We are infinite choice makers.

Some choices are made consciously, others unconsciously. Unconscious choices are often the result of conditioning. Over the years we develop repetitious and expected responses to the stimuli of our surroundings. Much like Pavlov's dogs, our reactions seem automatic, and we forget that we still choose how we react in every moment of our lives.

Making intentional choices often requires courage and resilience. It can be challenging to step out of your comfort zone or change ingrained habits. But it is precisely this willingness to embrace discomfort for long-term fulfillment that ultimately leads us toward personal growth and self-discovery.

Moreover, every choice carries consequences—some immediate and some far-reaching—that impact not only our own lives but also those around us. Understanding this interconnectedness reinforces the importance of mindful decision-making.

Thought, purposeful or habitual, is our reality. The conditions that surround us are merely outward manifestations of our innermost thoughts. As we change our thoughts, the outward material conditions change to remain in harmony with our new thoughts. If we want greater peace in our lives, we must develop a peaceful attitude. Our outer world is merely a reflection of our inner world.

Everything occurring around us at this moment is the result of choices we have made in the past. Our God-given endowment to choose our own thoughts, to influence our subconscious thinking, to communicate with God, and to realize our righteous goals and desires put us in control of our circumstances. We are always the ones who choose.

To more effectively live the forever formula of the eternal law of obedience, when we make choices, whatever those choices may be, we should ask ourselves these two questions:

1. "What are the consequences of the choice I am making?"

We will know immediately what these are through the light of Christ. God has given everyone the guidance of the Light of Truth, or the Spirit of Jesus Christ. If we listen closely to this spirit, we will be shown the truth.

The inspiration promised to all of us is the active agency by which the great accomplishments of our modern era have been realized. It is the same light by which the worlds were made and are maintained. It is the light of the sun and of all the heavenly bodies in the universe. And it is the light that will quicken our understanding.

> 2. "Will this choice bring success and happiness to me and those around me?"

If we can honestly answer yes to this question, then we should make that choice. If the answer is no or if the choice creates doubt and distress in our minds, then we shouldn't make that choice. It is no more complicated than that.

God has given us the privilege of choosing for ourselves, whether good or evil, but the results of our choices are in His hands.

We are always free to make choices, but we are never free from the consequences of those choices. Eventually, the time will come when we will be asked to face the consequences of our decisions.

We make our own path in life. We walk in the right or in the wrong. We tell the truth, or we lie and deceive. God has given us this right, and we can legislate and act as we please, but we are always in God's hands.

The results of our actions will be to His glory, and to the benefit of those who love Him. As we journey through life facing an ever-changing array of options at each crossroad, let's strive towards choices that resonate with authenticity, compassion, and purpose.

- # -

Thoughts & Inspiration

As we learn and understand spiritual laws, we can apply them to our personal success. If we violate them, we will suffer; if we obey them, we will be blessed. "Every obedience," wrote Sterling W. Sill in *Making the Most of Yourself*, "brings a blessing and every disobedience brings a suffering." [60] We can always depend on spiritual law.

We know that the sun will rise at a specific time every morning; we accept that electricity will always produce light under certain conditions. The laws of nature never vary. Imagine a scientist who is not able to depend on natural law. Imagine the engineer

---

[60] Sill, Sterling W., *Making the Most of Yourself*, p. 274.

disregarding the laws of physics. We cannot ignore natural laws and still be successful.

We begin to see that life operates on a set of principles that, when followed, make it easier to achieve our goals and find fulfillment. The law of attraction teaches us that maintaining positive thoughts and intentions can attract good things into our lives. Similarly, the principle of giving indicates that to receive abundance, one must first be willing to give freely.

Personal success is often linked closely with spiritual growth because our external reality tends to align more harmoniously with our inner state as we evolve deeper. This alignment manifests in various forms: professional achievements, harmonious relationships, physical health, and overall well-being.

Moreover, understanding spiritual laws helps us navigate challenges more gracefully. Instead of seeing obstacles as insurmountable problems or reasons for despair, we start viewing them as opportunities for growth and learning experiences designed to help us become more robust versions of ourselves.

Both natural and spiritual laws are made for our benefit, comfort, and safety. This allows us to align ourselves with the natural flow of the universe, fostering a sense of harmony and balance in our lives. Integrating these spiritual principles into our daily routines can enhance our emotional well-being, improve relationships, and achieve a more profound sense of fulfillment. God created law not to have a means to punish us but for our benefit. To be successful and happy, we must obey the laws and regulations that pertain to our activities.

"My religion," declared Amasa Lyman in 1857, "has become convenient to me, from the fact that I have found it adapted to everyday use. The happiness that it imparts—I do not care what part of man's existence or being you may talk about, or apply it to—the happiness it imparts it can impart every day. The bliss that can happify one hour of a man's being as a Saint, from a knowledge of the truth, and from the influence that truth will exert over him, will, upon the same principle, happify every hour of his life… This leads me to be happy continually; for it does away with a great many of the probabilities of a man's doing wrong, or being decoyed from the path of rectitude and virtue… *They have only to be diligent, faithful, true, and obedient to the requisitions of truth, to secure its presence with them continually…* We want to learn to get along comfortably with the little duties of life that we meet with every day—that make up the labor of every day. We want to learn to do those things right. You want to learn to be as holy at home by your firesides as you are when you go to church. You want to feel well, to enjoy the Spirit of God in every condition and relation of life." [61]

Job made a great statement about obedience. He said: "Though [God] slay me, yet will I trust him." [62] I wouldn't know how much Job understood his problems or what was happening to him, but he had faith that if he obeyed eternal law and did things right, he

---

[61] Lyman, Amasa, *Journal of Discourses* 5:35.
[62] Job 13:15.

would eventually understand the reasons later. Through righteous obedience to God, we develop the power of faith to carry us over the rough spots of life until we can understand and walk by sight again.

George Q. Cannon has stated: "I would rather have the blessings of God and His Holy Spirit resting upon me than to have a thousand things, however grand they may be, bestowed upon me and be destitute of the favor of God. That is the feeling I have. I know it is pleasant to have good things; I know it is pleasant to have beautiful surroundings; I know that it is a sweet thing for us to be able to supply our families' wants, and when they ask, to have it in our power to give; but there is something higher, something nobler, something better than this, and that is the favor of God. We should labor so as to have this, and at the same time *if we do, we may rest assured that all the rest will be added to us*. He will not leave us destitute. He will not deprive us of the blessings of the earth. On the contrary he will impart, and not only to us but to our children after us." [63]

To trust God under all circumstances is still our greatest success method. Even in the face of adversities, maintaining faith can provide us with the resilience and optimism needed to overcome challenges. By relying on divine guidance, we find a strength that surpasses our abilities and a sense of peace amidst the chaos. Ultimately, trusting God enables us to navigate life's complexities with greater clarity and purpose. If we openly and honestly obey spiritual law, we cannot fail.

People today have become confused. With the overwhelming influx of information from various sources – social media, news outlets, and personal opinions – it's becoming increasingly difficult to discern fact from fiction. As technology advances rapidly, many feel like they are constantly playing catch-up,

---

[63] Cannon, George Q., *Journal of Discourses* 26:321.

trying to stay informed while maintaining their mental well-being.

Amidst this flood of data, there is a growing sense of disconnect and isolation. Despite being more connected than ever through digital means, real human interaction is diminishing. People often find themselves in echo chambers where only similar viewpoints are reinforced, leading to community polarization and misunderstandings.

Many people don't know what to do with their lives and wish they could start over again. "If only I had known then what I know now," they say. Jesus lived a life without sin. He admonished us to do the same with his words: "Follow me." Obedience to this concept will guarantee our success. By diligent faith and genuine obedience to spiritual law, we will overcome our problems, even though we may not know how.

Through trust in the divine plan and persistent practice of spiritual principles, we align ourselves with a higher purpose. Challenges may appear insurmountable, yet by holding firm to our faith and continuing in righteous action, solutions will manifest in ways beyond our understanding.

In moments of doubt or adversity, it is crucial to remain steadfast and unwavering. The path may not always be clear, but each step forward under sacred guidance brings us closer to resolution. By nurturing our inner connection with the Divine and acting from a place of love and integrity, we create an environment where miracles unfold naturally.

God knows what is best. We must impress our minds that our most significant opportunity is to obey the rules God has established for our benefit. Then most of our problems will disappear.

Thoughts & Inspiration

THE VIRTUE OF OBEDIENCE

3 STEPS FOR PUTTING FORMULA

NUMBER THREE INTO EFFECT

I will extol the virtue of obedience in my personal life by committing to take the following steps:

1. I will become consciously aware of the choices I make daily.

2. I will ask myself two questions before every choice I make;
     a. What are the consequences of the choice I am making?
     b. Will this choice bring success and happiness to me and those around me?

3. I will be in tune with the Light of Truth and seek guidance in making choices through the Spirit of Christ. When a choice feels comfortable, I will proceed. I will pause

and seek a more precise answer when a choice raises doubts and discomfort.

Love and Service

"It is our duty to live in peace one with another".

Brigham Young (JD 15:64)

"We are shaped and fashioned by what we love."

Goethe

A lawyer approached Jesus and asked: "Master, which is the great commandment in the law?"

"Jesus said unto him, Thou shalt love the Lord thy God with all thy heart, and with all thy soul, and with all thy mind.

"This is the first and great commandment.

"And the second is like unto it, Thou shalt love thy neighbor as thyself.

"On these two commandments hang all the law and the prophets." [64]

The fourth Forever Formula for Success is the concept of loving others and

---

[64] Matthew 22:36-40.

giving service wherever it is needed. It is also known as the law of attraction. Through this law, we "attract" the physical manifestation of our desires. All the commandments of the Decalogue and all the other commandments hang upon this single great commandment: "Thou shalt love…"

The law of love is an eternal and fundamental principle that allows us to master adversity in human experience. It is inherent in all things, every system of philosophy, religion, and science. We cannot escape the power of the law of love.

Feeling imparts vitality to thought. The feeling is desire, and desire is love. When our thoughts become impregnated with love, we become invincible. The law of love gives our thoughts the power to correlate with the object of our desires.

Desire is the spiritual equivalent of gravity. It "attracts" or draws things together. When we attach desire to our thoughts, we increase their natural attractiveness. (In this context, attractiveness does not refer to physical beauty but the ability to attract.) Just as what we fear will come to pass, what we love will also come to pass. It is best to always focus on what we want and love and refuse to give any power to what we fear or dislike. We can and should learn to love entirely without fear. We should learn to go forward in faith and trust, knowing that everything in life contributes to our personal growth and fulfillment.[65]

We create the life we want by:

1. Consciously choosing what we think about.

2. Attaching fervent desire or love to those thoughts.

3. Believing that everything supports the materialization of what we design for ourselves.

The combination of thought and love forms an irresistible force. All natural laws are

---

[65] See Romans 8:28.

irresistible. The law of gravity, electricity, or any other law operates with mathematical exactitude. There is no variation. It is only the channel of distribution that may be imperfect. When a roof falls, we do not blame the collapse on some variation of the law of gravity. If the lights go out, we don't stop depending on the laws of electricity. And if the law of attraction seems unsatisfactory, evidenced by an inexperienced or uninformed person, we shouldn't assume that the greatest and most infallible law, the law on which the entire system of creation depends, has been suspended. Instead, we should conclude that a little more understanding of the law is required. The correct solution to a complex problem is not always readily and easily obtained.

In the Sermon on the Mount, Jesus teaches us to be meek, merciful, peacemakers, pure in heart, to suffer persecution for the sake of righteousness, not to swear, and to love our enemies. He also asks us to do good to those who hate us, pray for those who despitefully use us, forgive our fellowmen, judge not, and pray sincerely.

At the time of the Sermon on the Mount, the Jews had approximately 3,600 commandments written in their books of law. God has given numerous commandments to humanity, and all of them hang upon what Jesus called the first two commandments.

Paul taught that when we give to the needy, if we do not feel compassion for them, we do not have the pure love of Christ, which is charity. [66] He told us that when we have pure love, we feel a special affection toward everyone. We are patient and kind. We are not boastful or proud. We are not arrogant, selfish, or rude. When we have pure love, we do not rejoice in the evil others have done. Neither do we do good things just because it is in our own best interest. When we have charity, we are loyal and believe the best in others.

"If we merely have an assemblance of righteousness," stated Elder John Nicholson, "and our motives within are not of the godlike character they should be, that spirit will depart

---

[66] See 1 Corinthians 13:3.

from us, leaving us in greater darkness than before we possessed the Holy Spirit. *This Church is a brotherhood or it is nothing.*" [67]

We must carefully choose the thoughts, feelings, and desires that benefit ourselves and others because we will always reap what we sow, and we will always reap in greater abundance. Every thought, word, and action is a seed sown. Any judgment we place on people, events, circumstances, or conditions limits our capacity to grow because we focus on effects rather than causes.

Proper service can only be achieved when our actions are motivated by love. We are wasting our energy when we seek power or control over others. When we seek wealth or power for the sake of our selfish ego, we are expending our energy chasing an illusion of happiness instead of enjoying happiness in the moment. When we seek money for personal gain only, we cut off the energy flow. But when our actions are motivated by love, there is no

---

[67] Nicholson, John, *Journal of Discourses* 22:26.

wasted energy. When motivated by love, our energy multiplies and accumulates.

Abundance is the continual disposition of allowing God to act through us. This is demonstrated by our willingness to give and to serve. Service is wealth. If we can find a way to be of service, then we will attain wealth. The book How to Make More Money by Marvin Small reveals the secret to wealth creation in six simple words: "Find a need and fill it."

The laws of success are based on service. What we get is what we give. We should always consider it a privilege to give. "There can be no real success apart from service," writes an unknown author. "Success is but service visualized." Brian Tracy reminds us, "Successful people are always looking for opportunities to help others. Unsuccessful people are always asking, 'What's in it for me?'"

Those involved in marketing understand that people make money by making friends. They then enlarge their circle of friends by making money for them, helping them, and serving them. We can become money magnets by learning how to make money for others. The more we give, the more we will get.

Giving, in this sense, implies service. A banker gives money; a merchant offers goods; an author gives thoughts; and a worker gives skill; all have something to give. The more we give, the more we will get, and the more we get, the more we are able to give.

With our present economic system, there is a constant temptation to do the best we can for ourselves, even at the expense of another. The current system emphasizes selfishness.

"God did not create us for the purpose of striving for self alone," wrote George Q. Cannon, "and when we are rightly situated, under a proper system, our desires will naturally flow along, and we will find room for the exercise of every faculty of mind and body without endangering the salvation of our souls." [68]

---

[68] Cannon, George Q. *Journal of Discourses* 16:119.

Complying with the two great commandments to love when we are steeped in selfishness can be challenging. The more self-centered we are, the less interested we become in God's things. We tend to define our relationship with Him in terms of "What has He done for me lately?" instead of seeing ways in which we can be of service.

Selfishness precedes self-pity, and self-pity is void of compassion, empathy, or service to others. It then becomes increasingly difficult to give of ourselves and to rid ourselves of selfish desires and thoughts. But when we genuinely love someone, we will find that nothing we do for that person is a hardship.

Whatever we want out of life for ourselves, we should also affirm for others.

This way, we help the person we want to bless, and, at the same time, we bless ourselves. Remember that we reap what we sow. If the desires we hold for another are for love and health, those same desires will return to us like bread cast on the water; but if we harbor thoughts or feelings of fear, worry, jealousy, anger, or hate, we will reap those very same results in our own lives.

It is axiomatic that "two things cannot exist in the same place at the same time." The same is true in the mental and spiritual worlds. We can substitute thoughts of love, courage, power, self-reliance, and confidence for those of hatred, fear, lack, and limitation.

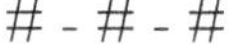

- # -

Thoughts & Inspiration

One way we can apply the principles of the second great commandment is to be willing to work at improving troubled relationships. Occasionally, we all have difficulties in relationships, and we are obligated to work them out. The Savior said, "Moreover if thy brother shall trespass against thee, go and tell his fault between thee and him alone: if he shall hear thee, thou hast gained thy brother."[69]

Taking the initiative to repair or strengthen a relationship requires love and courage. It means putting in the effort and facing potential vulnerabilities head-on. This might involve honest communication, active listening, and sometimes making compromises.

---

[69] Matthew 18:15.

It also requires patience, as rebuilding or enhancing trust doesn't happen overnight. By prioritizing the relationship and committing to work through challenges, you can build a stronger bond that withstands future obstacles. Remember, every meaningful relationship involves two people ready to give their best to each other, even during tough times.

At a Seventies' conference in 1853, Ezra T. Benson counseled that we should "have respect and kindness for each other; let us feel well towards each other, speak good things to each other, and of each other, for this is the way Saints should live. When we take this course we shall feel right. When I feel like blessing my brethren, like lifting them up, and exalting them in my feelings, I feel first-rate myself." [70]

Every emotion and every thought is a choice. People often allow previous experiences and present conditions to determine what they feel and think. They end

---

[70] Benson, Ezra T., *Journal of Discourses* 2:352.

up being controlled. When we exercise our freedom of choice, we are in control. We can shape our lives according to our desires and values. Each decision we make reflects our personal journey, goals, and aspirations. By embracing this autonomy, we foster a sense of responsibility toward ourselves and others, acknowledging that each action contributes to the broader tapestry of society.

Taking ownership of our choices also empowers us to learn from experiences – both successes and failures. As we navigate different life paths, deriving lessons from every step helps us grow more resilient and adaptable.

Conscious choice produces results that are in harmony with our personal desires. Every action that is not in harmony with truth, whether through ignorance or design, will result in discord. When we choose to do those things that empower us and others, we will find success and happiness. Harmony within us will always produce harmonious conditions in the world around us.

"The fruits of the Spirit of God," stated John Taylor, "are love, peace, joy, gentleness, long-suffering, kindness, affection, and everything that is good and amiable. The fruits of the spirit of the devil are envy, hatred, malice, irritableness, everything that tends to destroy mankind, and to make them feel uncomfortable and unhappy. The fruits of the Spirit of God are love, and peace, and joy in the Holy Ghost; and the man that says he loves God and hateth his brother is a liar, and the truth is not in him. I do not care who he may be, or what his name, or where he lives." [71]

Along those same lines Elder John Nicholson advised: "Let the hand of fellowship be extended to him who is cast down, that he may be comforted. Surround him with a halo of love and friendship, and let him know that he is not forgotten, and the Lord will remember those who act this brotherly part." [72]

---

[71] Taylor, John, *Journal of Discourses* 20:141.
[72] Nicholson, John, *Journal of Discourses* 22:26.

God will bless us to be better neighbors if we openly and sincerely acknowledge our brotherhood with others as more than just a sweet-sounding slogan. If we don't love our neighbor as ourselves, we may one day betray him just as we betray ourselves when we don't live by the highest principles that we know. True love for another is a journey that can be filled with great enjoyment and gratification, even in the early stages. It's a journey that, while it may take most of us a lifetime to find, is filled with hope and promise.

If we are to have this love of which the Savior spoke, it must begin in our homes and carry over into our daily lives. A happy marriage is never handed to a couple on a silver platter. It is something that must be built and repaired continually. A happy marriage is never handed to a couple on a silver platter. It is something that must be constructed and repaired continually.

If we think of the other's comforts, needs, and happiness in our relationships, if we are determined to see the best in the other, and if we try to understand and express love for each other, then true love and harmony will exist in the home. Understanding is a key component of this harmony, allowing us to truly connect with our loved ones.

As mentioned previously, the second Forever Formula for Success is the principle of sacrifice. It is one of the fundamental laws of eternal progress. If one marriage partner sacrifices personal interests to provide for the welfare and happiness of the other partner, both will be fulfilled and happy. If one partner promotes personal interest at the expense of the partner's interests, desires, or happiness, discord and contention will result.

"I also think it is our duty, upon the principles of righteousness, to please each other as far as we can," advised Daniel H. Wells. "…strive to please each other, instead of pursuing an opposite course, or one that is calculated to harass and injure each other's feelings… and knowing that in all righteousness we should seek to build each other up. We should seek to have within ourselves that spirit and feeling which will produce the most happiness and prosperity." [73]

The only doctrine required to ensure a happy relationship is: *Love Each Other* – three simple words. Yet, within those three simple words lies an immense depth of commitment, understanding, and action. To love each other means communicating openly and honestly, such as sharing your feelings without fear of judgment or having regular check-ins about your relationship. It involves supporting one another through challenges, like being there for each other during tough times or helping each other achieve personal goals. And appreciating each person's unique qualities, by acknowledging and celebrating what makes your partner special. It involves patience during difficult times and celebrating successes together. A couple forms a strong foundation that can weather any storm by consistently practicing empathy, respect, and kindness— always seeking common ground even amidst

---

[73] Wells, Daniel H., *Journal of Discourses* 9:46.

differences. In essence, loving each other is a feeling as well as a daily practice of choosing connection over conflict.

If we were to apply the principle of love, sacrifice for each other, and strive to make each other happy, we would have little trouble in our relationships. The importance and value of being courteous, kind, considerate, and polite to others must be emphasized.

If our lives seem void of real love, we should realize that the only way we get love is by giving love. The more we give, the more we will get. This reciprocity of love should give us hope and encourage us to keep giving. We can best give love to others when we have first filled ourselves with it. We can become a love magnet and have love flow effortlessly and in ever-increasing measure.

"But if we withhold our hand," cautioned Amasa Lyman, "and do not bless our brethren and sisters as we should, will God hear us when we pray to him? I tell you he will not. We might pray until we were so hoarse that we could not speak; we might pray in thunder tones, till our prayers could be heard from one end of the continent to the other, and still he would not listen to us. He has told us what spirit we should pray in and how we should act towards those around us. Then *let us go and cultivate these things in our homes, in our family circles: for this is the most effectual way to carry out these principles.*" [74]

No one can fulfill the two great commandments all the time, but we can, by seriously trying, find greater joy, success, happiness, and friendship as we go through life. If we look for the best in others, our friends, neighbors, wives, husbands, and children, they will soon appear to be the most wonderful people on earth. When we focus on their virtues, we magnify their goodness in our eyes and encourage positive behavior. This perspective allows us to cultivate love, understanding, and harmony in our relationships.

---

[74] Lyman, Amasa, *Journal of Discourses* 5:348.

Conversely, if we look for weaknesses and faults and focus solely on them, these same people will seem despicable. Dwelling on faults and shortcomings may foster negativity and discord. Therefore, choosing to seek out the best not only uplifts others but also enriches our own lives with joy and deeper connections. In doing so, we contribute to a more compassionate and caring world where everyone has an opportunity to shine.

"While we have the privilege of speaking to each other," advises Brigham Young, "let us speak words of comfort and consolation. When you are influenced by the Spirit of holiness and purity, let your light shine; but if you are tired and tempted and buffeted by Satan, keep your thoughts to yourself—keep your mouths closed; for speaking produces fruit, either of a good or evil character." [75]

The kind of love which attracts success does not allow us to hold grudges or ill feelings.

---

[75] Young, Brigham, *Journal of Discourses* 7:268.

Ill feelings canker the soul and crowd out love. Likewise, we hurt ourselves by holding grudges. We often see employers, co-workers, and members of clubs and churches criticizing one another and trying to expand on others' weaknesses to belittle them. When we love one another as the Lord loves us, this friction disappears, and confidence, happiness, and success replace it.

Brigham Young directs us to: "Frame your lives according to the precepts of the Gospel. Let your deal, walk, and conversation be that upon which an angel can look with pleasure. And in all your social communications, or whatever your associations are, let all the dark, discontented, murmuring, unhappy, miserable feelings—all the evil fruit of the mind, fall from the tree in silence and unnoticed; and let it perish, without taking it up to present to your neighbors. But when you have joy and happiness, light and intelligence, truth and virtue, offer that fruit abundantly to your neighbors, and it will do them good, and so strengthen the hands of your fellow-beings." [76]

Ask yourself these questions:

1. Am I trying to apply the principle of love toward all others?

2. Am I patient, kind, generous, unselfish, and sincere?

3. Do I try to put myself in the other person's place, acting toward them as I would like to be treated if I were in a similar situation?

"Let us remember that we have all got to show by our works that we are worthy of this life and of this salvation which is now offered," advised Lorenzo Snow. "Now when a man is not willing to sacrifice for the benefit of his brethren, and when he knows that he trespasses upon the feelings of his brethren, and yet he has not that love which will enable him to make satisfaction, that man is not right

---

[76] Young, Brigham, *Journal of Discourses* 7:269.

before the Lord, and where is the love of that individual for his brother?”

We need to strive to always focus on what we want, and we should want for others those blessings we want for ourselves. If we desire negatives for another person, *we must first think those negative thoughts, and those thoughts are ours and will attract into our lives what we are thinking about.*

THOUGHTS & INSPIRATION

The extended golden rule says much more than "do unto others as you would have them do unto you." It is based on the natural laws of cause and effect. We must wish for others what we desire for ourselves.

It expands this idea by incorporating the concepts of understanding and empathy. Instead of merely treating others how you would like to be treated, it encourages you to consider their unique perspectives, needs, and circumstances. This deeper consideration fosters more meaningful connections and promotes greater compassion and respect among individuals.

By embracing the extended golden rule, you practice kindness and actively engage in creating a more empathetic and harmonious community. It challenges you to look beyond your experiences and understand what others might value or require. This shift towards an outward-focused mindset can lead to richer interpersonal relationships and contribute significantly to social cohesion.

The extended golden rule goes beyond fundamental reciprocity; it's about cultivating a relationship in which mutual respect and genuine care for one another are fundamental principles guiding our interactions.

This is the origin of actual service.

Give in order to get. The seeds we plant will be the fruit we reap. All things replicate after their kind. We need to think only of what is best for us and others. We should always desire for others only those same things we choose for ourselves.

The Savior's life reflects His pure love for all humanity. He even gave His life, not just for us but for the most despicable and hateful among us. He has commanded us to love one another as He has loved us. When we have pure love for those around us, we exhibit genuine concern and heartfelt compassion.

"Modeling" others has become a popular success technique of our time. The concept originates from the idea that by studying and replicating successful individuals' behaviors, strategies, and thought processes, one can achieve similar levels of success in one's own life. This technique is rooted in various fields, such as psychology, business, sports coaching, and self-help literature. Advocates argue that by identifying key patterns and practices employed by high achievers—from daily routines to specific skills—they can streamline their path to excellence.

Modeling others involves more than mere imitation; it requires a deep understanding of why specific actions lead to success. Effective modeling demands thorough observation and sometimes direct mentorship or guidance from the role models.

The Savior gave us the example of His life to follow. He had perfect love, and He showed us how we should love. By modeling His example, our fellow humans' spiritual and physical needs become as important to us as our own. Through acts of kindness, charity, and empathy, we strive to positively impact their lives. By doing so, we demonstrate the same love and compassion that Jesus taught.

Our actions speak louder than words, showing our commitment to following His teachings in every aspect of our lives. Whether through volunteering, offering support during difficult moments, or simply sharing a friendly smile, we embody the principles of service and love central to our faith. Through these efforts, we help others and grow spiritually as we draw closer to living out the true message of Christianity.

Shortly before He gave His life for us, Jesus said: "This is my commandment, That ye love one another as I have loved you. Greater love hath no man than this, that a man lay down his life for his friends." [77] It may not be

---

[77] John 15:12, 13.

necessary for us to give our lives as the Savior did, but we can practice and apply the law of love and service when we follow His example and teachings, model His life, and try to be like Him.

Thoughts & Inspiration

LOVE AND SERVICE

3 STEPS FOR PUTTING FORMULA

NUMBER FOUR INTO EFFECT

The Savior was our example of how to treat others. He despised wickedness, but He loved the sinner despite his sins. He had compassion for children, the elderly, the poor, and the needy. He had such great love that He could beg our Heavenly Father to forgive the soldiers who were driving nails into His hands and feet. We must learn to feel toward others as Jesus did.

The Savior taught that we must love others as we love ourselves. And to love ourselves, we must respect and trust ourselves. We will only come to love ourselves when we can feel the deep, comforting assurance that Jesus truly loves us.

I will love and serve others in my personal life by making a commitment to take the following steps:

1. I will learn to love myself. As I come to love myself, my love for others will increase. I will not think that I am better than other people. I will have patience with their faults.

2. I will learn to love my neighbor. When I feel uncharitable toward anyone, I will pray to have those feelings removed.

3. I will study the life of Jesus Christ, learn what He did in certain situations, and then do the same things when I am in similar situations. The better I know God, the more disposed I will be to look with compassion on others.

The Principle of Faith

"Goals are as essential to success as air is to life."

David Schwartz

"Without faith a man can do nothing; with it all things are possible."

Sir William Osler

The fifth Forever Formula for Success is the principle of faith. It involves developing worthy goals and desires. *The greatest discovery we can make in this life is finding the real meaning of faith.*

The commanding strength of faith is its capacity to entice us to action. Faith adds significance to our beliefs and vitality to our knowledge. When belief develops into conviction and becomes a motivating force, it has evolved into faith. Faith is not an inert mental belief but an active conviction of the heart.

Orson Pratt tells us: "It is through faith we are made partakers of these glorious blessings; for by faith all the blessings promised are to be obtained." [78]

There are two specific aspects to faith. One of these is the faith we have in Christ.

Jesus said, "Ye believe in God, believe also in me." [79] Only through faith in Christ can we find peace and abundance in this life. Peter proclaimed, "There is none other name under heaven given among men, whereby we must be saved." [80]

"What is the first condition required of the human family?" asks Orson Pratt. "It is to believe in Jesus Christ as the true redeemer, and in his Father as the true God. This condition stands before repentance, baptism, the sacrament, or keeping the Sabbath day holy… This faith or belief is the first principle of the Gospel." [81]

---

[78] Pratt, Orson, *Journal of Discourses* 25:146.
[79] John 14:1.
[80] Acts 4:12.
[81] Pratt, Orson, *Journal of Discourses* 7:258, 259.

We must have faith in Jesus Christ. Many scriptures illustrate this point, but the conclusive words of the Savior Himself are: "If ye believe not that I am he, ye shall die in your sins." [82] We develop our faith in Him when we hear, accept, and begin to follow Christ's words. We do not need to know all the answers or understand the entire Gospel before we begin to demonstrate our faith.

The other aspect of faith is the substance or condition of things hoped for and the evidence of things not seen.[83] Simply expressed, it is continuing to do something until we succeed and trying until we get it right.

When we have faith, *we act as if we have knowledge*—as if the thing we have faith in is already an established fact. Without faith in the autumn harvest, we would not plant in the spring. Faith is the foundation of hope. It incorporates all our aspirations and ambitions

---

[82] John 8:24.
[83] Hebrews 11:1.

for the future. *When faith is founded in truth, it will always be verified in experience.*

In his book *Turning Faith into Power*, Richard Nelson explains, "Faith is the substance of things hoped for, the *evidence* of things not seen." [84] **Faith is evidence!** It is "the *assertion* of facts that are otherwise not evident and cannot be proven." [85]

We cannot effectively produce our life's desires without faith. Faith moves our hopes and desires into the realm of realization and achievement. Faith enables us to rise above the daily problems and challenges of life. Faith destroys doubt and replaces it with confidence. It applies to every condition of success.

Faith is a fundamental power of the spiritual world. We know the power of electricity and gravity by their effect on material things and use them endlessly and efficiently. Although we do not understand the

---

[84] Ibid.
[85] Nelson, S. Richard, *Turning Faith into Power*, p. 16.

exact nature of faith, we know its attributes and relationships. They are as follows:

1. Faith is active. Eliminate the characteristic of action from faith, and it becomes mere belief. Faith is belief in action. A child believes it can walk and will persist until it does. Faith in our success will ensure that we continue until we succeed. Faith is the conviction that compels us to action.

"Let this faith be distributed, and it makes all things easy," wrote Brigham Young. "It is with the mental powers as it is with the physical, and that is why I wish you to consider the matter, and why I lay those things before you. Let the Latter-day Saints have faith and works." [86]

2. Faith looks to the future. Faith extends from the past through the present and into the future. Faith surpasses knowledge because knowledge is centered on experience and past observations. Our choices are infinite.

---

[86] Young, Brigham, *Journal of Discourses* 3:46.

We can be, do, and have anything we desire. By governing our thought forces today, we create the success that will materialize in our lives in the future.

3. Faith goes hand-in-hand with knowledge. Faith augments knowledge, and knowledge, when rightly applied, creates more effective faith.

"Belief is inherent in the creature," explains Brigham Young, "implanted within him for his use and benefit—to believe or disbelieve. Your own experience may satisfy you that faith is not brought into requisition by the presentation of either facts or falsehoods to the external senses, or to the inward perceptions of the mind. If we speak of faith in the abstract, it is the power of God by which the worlds are and were made, and it is a gift of God to those who believe and obey his commandments." [87]

---

[87] Young, Brigham, *Journal of Discourses* 8:259.

4. Faith is explicit. It is related to meaning, activity, and function. We do not just have faith; we have faith in specific things. Faith has power when it is equated to principles, laws, and relationships.

5. Faith is operative. Without faith, life as we know it would not exist. Banks would not exist, businesses would not be established, students would not attend school, and contracts would not be signed. Faith is the lifeblood of all practical and meaningful relationships.

"The faith of the Latter-day Saints is a living principle," wrote John Morgan. "A Latter-day Saint devoid of the principle of faith would be an anomaly—in fact such an one could not be a Latter-day Saint; for it requires faith in the God of Israel to stand the tests that they are called upon to pass through. Yet calmly and quietly, deliberately, with full confidence in Jehovah, they can go forth in the discharge of their duties as they understand them, believing that in the outcome, God will be their friend and protector in the future as

He has been in the past; as He brought them through the trials and tribulations of days gone by, so will He do in the future. This principle of faith… was certainly a most important one, and it is one without which it would be impossible for the Latter-day Saints to have succeeded." [88]

6. Faith is confidence. It is a feeling of inner certainty. It is the assurance born of conviction.

"If men are faithful," wrote Brigham Young, "the time will come when they will possess the power and the knowledge to obtain, organize, bring into existence, and to own." [89]

7. Faith is the mainspring of inventiveness. Faith drives us to solve problems. Through faith, we ask questions, believing that the answers will be found.

---

[88] Morgan, John, *Journal of Discourses* 25:76.
[89] Young, Brigham, *Journal of Discourses* 2:304.

8. Faith is the road to success, the road to the answers to life's compelling questions. Faith offers us purpose and meaning in life.

Faith in the Gospel of Jesus Christ, or anything else, means assimilating it into our lives and living it. It is more than just accepting something to be true. The misfortune of having only belief is that belief alone does not reach the gospel objectives of abundant living, growth, and achievement. These come only through faith, each requiring a personal application of the laws and principles through work and effort. Faith is you in action.

- # -

Thoughts & Inspiration

The principle of faith, as demonstrated by most successful individuals, will literally and without fail bring us the circumstances, surroundings, and experiences in life that fit our habitual, characteristic, and predominant mental attitude. These successful people hold ideals of the pure conditions they wish to achieve and constantly visualize the next step necessary to reach their ideal.

Faith calls into existence what does not exist in the objective world. This process is aided through visualization.

The entire universe is an act of creative visualization. We share in this same power of creative visualization. Anything we want in life can be brought into manifestation by first visualizing. The creative process is:

1. Conceptualization.
2. Visualization.
3. Affirmation.
4. Faith, and
5. Manifestation.

Our ability to conceptualize and then visualize what we most desire creates our reality.

The first step is conceptualization, which simply means having a clear idea or plan to build upon. When we picture something in our minds (visualize), we are sowing a seed. But before we sow that seed, we should decide what we want to harvest. If you want to grow tomatoes, don't plant a pumpkin seed. This is conceptualization.

Alfred A. Montapert stated: "What do I really want? This is one of the most important questions you will ever ask yourself. Spell out your desires."

Next is the process of visualization. Visualization is making mental images. The image we hold in our minds is the model which shapes our future. The universe was thought into shape before it ever became a material fact.[90] If we are willing to follow the example of the Great Architect of the universe, our thoughts will take physical form, just as the universe took physical form.

"Where there is no vision, the people perish." [91]

As we grow more aware of the lavish power of our inner world, we can begin to draw on this power to apply and develop greater possibilities, which this discernment has realized. What we become conscious of is invariably brought into tangible expression and evidenced in the physical world. Each of us is a channel through which this eternal energy manifests. Our ability to think is our ability to act. What we think about is what we create or produce in the material world. The ability to eliminate undesirable and imperfect conditions depends on our mental actions. Our mental action, in turn, depends on our awareness of

---

90 See Moses 3:5.
91 Proverbs 29:18.

the power of faith. Nothing can permanently impede our eternal progress or stand in the way of our perfect success when we apply spiritually and scientifically correct thought methods and principles.

Life is constantly testing our level of commitment. The most significant rewards are obtained by those who demonstrate a never-ending commitment to act until they achieve. This level of determination can move mountains if it is constant and consistent. A goal must fill us with positive emotion; we must ardently desire its fulfillment. The more intensely we feel about an idea or a goal, the more assuredly it will guide us to its fulfillment.

People seldom ever begin to push toward their goals if they fear failure. Or they start pursuing a goal but give up too soon.

The delightful piano-playing comedian Victor Borge tells of his grandfather inventing unsuccessful products. Borge says his grandfather invented 1-up, 2-up, 3-up, 4-up, 5-up, 6-up and then quit. "If he had only known," laments Mr. Borge, "how close he came." Even though we are on track to achieve what we desire, we must maintain the necessary persistence and patience if we are going to realize success.

If I asked you what your current goal is, could you tell me? Is your goal clear and concise in your mind? Is it written down in your day planner or journal, and do you read it daily? When I ask people about their goals, they usually answer in vague generalities. They say things like sound health, happiness, exaltation, or lots of money. However, the more precisely and clearly defined a goal, the more natural it will become. The more natural it is, the more readily attainable it becomes.

Goal setting should be followed by developing a plan and taking massive and consistent action toward its fulfillment. The power to act is already ours. When we fail to act on our goals, we likely do not have goals that inspire us. Nothing was ever achieved by only being interested in its achievement. We must be committed.

The goal-setting process is similar to our eyesight. We gain greater clarity and understanding the closer we come to our destination, not only of the goal itself but the fine points of its achievement. Write down everything you can think of that you want to have happen in your life. When you've listed all your physical, spiritual, social, emotional, intellectual, and financial desires, review the list, prioritizing each item in order of importance. Then, make item number one your present goal. Whenever we set goals, we commit to the need that all human beings have for eternal progression.

People constantly put off their joy and happiness. They forget that this is the day of our probation.[92] They believe that "someday," after they have accomplished something, they will be able to enjoy life to its fullest. I mentioned earlier that success is the *progressive* realization of a worthy goal and that our direction is more critical than individual results.

------

[92] See Alma 12:24.

Setting goals is not what truly matters. What truly matters is the quality of life we experience and what we become along the way.

Our goals, whatever they are, significantly affect us. If we do not consciously plant desirable seeds in the gardens of our minds, we will end up with weeds. The weeds are automatic; we do not need to work at achieving them. But if we want to discover the unlimited potential and possibility within us, we must uncover a goal grand enough to challenge us to excel beyond our limitations to find our true potential. The size and quality of our goals, not our present circumstances, represent our potential.

Challenged by the Soviet Union's initial Sputnik satellite launch, President Kennedy determined that the United States would put a man on the moon. At the time, fully 50% of the required technology did not exist. The decision to set the goal, accept its possibility, and accomplish it produced the scientific and technological innovations necessary to make the goal a reality. The spin-offs from these new technologies have changed our lives forever.

In the same sense, when we decide to achieve any goal in our personal lives, it is not necessary that we already have the education, money, tools, or know-how to accomplish the goal. It is, however, necessary that we believe in our ability to achieve and persist in accomplishing that goal. All the necessary components will come together along the way to produce a successful outcome that also benefits others in numerous ways.

Our subconscious does not consider time or space. It can only comprehend the present moment. Therefore, it is important to affirm and visualize goals as already existing and completed in the present.

Grateful appreciation in advance for achieving our goals is one of the best "tricks" to play on the subconscious. Thankfulness and gratitude confirm to the subconscious that it had better catch up with reality quickly. If we are thankful for something we don't have, it will show up. We should also be grateful for everything we *do* have in life.

"I do not know of anything," wrote the prophet Brigham Young, "excepting the unpardonable sin, that is greater than the sin of ingratitude." [93]

Gratitude is one of the most significant affirmations we can make. It shifts our attention from what we lack to the abundance that already exists in our lives. When we actively express gratitude, we train our minds to focus on positivity and recognize the small blessings around us.

This practice not only improves our overall mood but also strengthens relationships by fostering appreciation and warmth between people. Moreover, many psychological studies have demonstrated that consistent expressions of gratitude are linked to increased levels of happiness and well-being. By making it a habit to regularly acknowledge what we're thankful

---

[93] Young, Brigham, *Journal of Discourses* 14:277.

for, we cultivate a more fulfilling and enriched life.

Gratitude for something we anticipate as though we already have it comes from faith, from knowing that when we ask, we shall receive. We are simply saying "thank you" for something we have yet to receive, and consequently, we make it so.

If you are thankful for anything, you might as well be grateful for everything. All the events, circumstances, and conditions that brought you to where you are today were necessary. Accept all occurrences as positive steps on the path to success.

- # -

Thoughts & Inspiration

Faith, the bedrock of our achievements, is a force that empowers us, making us capable of persevering, facing challenges, and conquering any obstacle. It's not just a belief in something greater, but also a trust in our own abilities and potential. It's the driving force that propels us forward when the odds seem insurmountable and keeps us grounded in times of triumph.

Having the ideal in mind and having visualized it, we must release it and believe it is already ours. This is the key to attaining our desires. By releasing the ideal and trusting in its manifestation, we align ourselves with the natural flow of life. Our focus shifts from a position of wanting or needing to one of gratitude and acceptance, as if what we've desired is already part of our reality. This shift elevates our mindset and attunes us to opportunities and actions that bring us closer to realizing our goals. We can develop greater faith by believing daily in ourselves and where we are going.

It is necessary for us to read our written goals every day and to visualize those goals as being already completed. We are also required to persist and be patient. Consider how long you would give a baby to learn how to walk. Remember that persistence is key; everyone progresses at their own pace. Just as you wouldn't rush a baby learning to walk, be patient with yourself and remain dedicated, regardless of the obstacles. Consistent effort will eventually lead to success. Celebrate small milestones along the way, and keep your eyes on the ultimate objective. Continue to work at your goal until it is yours.

We must exercise our faith. Our minds should be challenged, and our faith put to the test. Even if our faith is small at first, like a seed planted in the heart, its influence and effect may not be immediately noticeable. But with patience and persistence, the seed will eventually begin to sprout and grow. If nurtured, it will continue to grow until it becomes a mighty tree that fills us with light, wisdom, knowledge, and the gifts and qualifications necessary to make us perfect.

George Q. Cannon has advised us to "seek for the faith once delivered to the Saints. I know that faith will grow in you, and it should grow in you and you should instill it into your children, that it may be a fixed principle with them, that we whom God has called from the nations of the earth may be the nucleus of a faith that shall be disseminated until there shall be found amongst us the faith once given to Saints, and until a race shall spring from us who, like the mighty of ancient days, shall, through faith stop the mouths of lions, put to flight the armies of the aliens, quench the violence of fire and raise their dead to life; until the darkness that enshrouded us and our fathers shall be known no more, and we be prepared for an eternal residence in His presence." [94]

---

[94] Cannon, George Q., *Journal of Discourses* 15:376.

Thoughts & Inspiration

THE PRINCIPLE OF FAITH

3 STEPS FOR PUTTING FORMULA

NUMBER FIVE INTO EFFECT

I will put the principle of faith into effect in my personal life by committing to take the following steps:

1. I will clearly define my goals using specific and measurable terms. I will write down each goal along with a plan for its achievement and commit to reviewing my list daily, thereby staying committed and focused on my journey.

2. Through faith, I will become conscious of my inner power and draw on that power by conceptualizing and visualizing what I desire, thereby feeling inspired and motivated by the empowerment it brings.

3. I will express gratitude for what I do not yet have but am working to accomplish. This could be through daily prayer, affirmations, writing in a gratitude journal,

or simply acknowledging the progress I've made toward my goals.

Seek First the Kingdom of God

"I want to know God's thoughts...the rest are details."

Albert Einstein

The sixth Forever Formula for Success is seeking first the kingdom of God. It means that we know and understand the mind and will of God. This strategy does not imply that we should abandon our personal intentions of creating the conditions we desire. Instead, we turn those desires over to the wisdom of an all-knowing God and trust that He will cause "all things to work together for your good." [95]

Seeking the kingdom of God first is essential because we must find the kingdom before we can have anything added to it. "Seek ye first the kingdom of God, and his righteousness, and all these things shall be added unto you." [96] "All these things" does not mean anything we want or think we want.

[95] D&C 105:40.
[96] Matthew 6:33.

However, it includes everything for our personal good and success. Having everything we want or ask for is not always good for us. Part of our training and the probation of our lives requires that we discipline ourselves to want only those things that are right for us and to learn to discern between what is suitable for us and what is wrong.

"Wherefore, the Lord God gave unto man that he should act for himself… wherefore, men are free according to the flesh; and *all things are given them which are expedient unto man.*" [97]

If we serve the Lord in His way, we are traveling along a path leading us to the most tremendous success and joy we could experience in this life. Some of God's children want to change the rules and serve Him only in their own way. But to progress, enjoy success and happiness, and access the Spirit of the Lord, we must serve Him in *His* way.

---

[97] 2 Nephi 2:16, 27.

"And thou... hast not sought thine own life, but hast sought my will, and to keep my commandments.

"And now, because thou hast done this with unwearyingness, *behold, I will bless thee forever; and I will make thee mighty in word and in deed, in faith and in works; yea, even that all things shall be done unto thee according to thy word.*" [98]

Free agency is an eternal principle. It has always existed. Without it, God could not be God. The mastery of personal development and the power that moves us toward perfection is determined by freedom of choice. Without this eternal principle, there would be no progression. [99]

Genuine success is the capacity to have whatever we want, whenever we want it, and with the least effort. This success is promised in the Lord's words to His disciples:

"Ask, and it shall be given you; seek, and ye shall find; knock, and it shall be opened unto you;

"For every one that asketh receiveth; and to him that knocketh it shall be opened." [100]

Have you ever noticed what happens when you drop a pebble into a pond? Concentric circles appear as visible ripples on the surface of the pond. Introducing a frequency vibration stimulates the water, creating this wave pattern. If two pebbles are dropped into the pond, each will create its own wave pattern. At the point where they interact, they make what is known as an interference pattern.

Our thoughts, electrical impulses in the brain, also create a wave pattern that emanates outward in similar concentric circles. At the same time, a constant frequency wave pattern emanates from the mind of God. When our thoughts intersect and interact with the

---

[100] Matthew 6:7, 8.

thoughts of God, a harmonic interference pattern is created.

Inspiration is the ability to adjust the individual mind to the mind and will of God. When our thoughts and desires are in harmony with the thoughts and desires of God, we have created the condition where we can have all things done according to our word.

"If men would search deep into their own hearts," advised Lorenzo Snow, "they would discover that their desires and feelings, and in fact many things which they do and say, are not in accordance with the mind and will of the Lord." [101]

God is omnipotent; there is no limit to what He can do. Our degree of success in life is decided by the characteristics of our desires and the choices we make. If the nature of our desires is in harmony with natural law and with the mind and will of God, the physical manifestation of our desires will eventually be

---

[101] Snow, Lorenzo, *Journal of Discourses* 5:64.

revealed in our lives. This alignment with God's will should guide us and reassure us that we are on the right path to success.

- # -

Thoughts & Inspiration

One aspect by which we measure success, and one that we are constantly seeking, is security. Our attachment to money is a sign of our insecurities. We believe that when we have made a million dollars, or two, or ten, then we will feel secure. We will be financially independent. We will be able to retire and finally have the means and security to do everything we would like to do. But this doesn't happen. The pursuit of this illusion of security is somewhat ephemeral. People will seek security for an entire lifetime and never find it. It remains elusive because security can never come from money alone.

However, security can be discovered in the empowering embrace of spiritual laws. These laws, often referred to as the laws of God, are the fundamental principles that govern the universe and guide us in all aspects of life. As John Taylor eloquently put it, God "is going to establish a reign of righteousness and introduce a correct form of government, even the government of God, the laws of God, the revelations of God to guide and direct in all things: He will be our guide in philosophy, in politics, in agriculture, in science, in art, and in everything that is calculated to enlighten and impart intelligence, and give knowledge of the laws of nations, of the laws of nature, of matter, and of laws that regulate all things pertaining to time and to eternity." [102]

God creates, upholds, and quickens the universe. As His children, we have access to a direct communication link with God. This link is not a physical one, but a spiritual connection that we can strengthen through prayer, meditation, and living in alignment with spiritual laws. Effectively accessing that communication link and bringing ourselves into harmony with it affords us the complete

---

[102] Taylor, John, *Journal of Discourses* 11:26.

capacity and endowment to create our reality. We can take control of our personal lives and circumstances. We can create the health, happiness, and abundance we desire. Our eternal happiness and success are placed within our control instead of being at the mercy of external or capricious influences.

Through prayer, we are linked with God and associated with heaven's infinite creative forces. Our personal power is determined by how attuned we are to God's mind and will. By learning to understand and control our own personal power, we find our ability to create the desires of our lives. If we live the spirit of these laws until they become habitual, they will become ours by right. It will then be impossible to keep them from us.

Understanding God's mind and will enables us to plan our lives with courage and fearlessly execute our plans because we gain a knowledge and understanding of the source of all power. This understanding will determine and shape the course of our lives forever. It will bring us into contact with all that is best and most desirable. We can achieve, accomplish, and attain anything we desire by becoming in tune with the will of heaven.

"Now, when a person receives intelligence from the Lord," wrote Lorenzo Snow, "and is willing to communicate that for the benefit of the people, he will receive continual additions to that intelligence; *and there is no end to his increase so long as he will hold fast to the faith of the Lord Jesus Christ.*"[103]

We choose our personal beliefs, and those beliefs directly affect our lifestyle. We choose our actions, and our actions always have consequences. This realization empowers us to take responsibility for our entire reality. It's a powerful reminder that we are in control of our beliefs and actions, and therefore, our destiny.

This being the case, we can change our world simply by changing our minds. If we are not altogether pleased with the circumstances

---

[103] Snow, Lorenzo, *Journal of Discourses* 5:64.

of our present situation, we can change our lives by changing our thoughts and beliefs. This understanding offers a hopeful and optimistic perspective, showing that change is always within our reach.

Every belief, emotion, thought, and action is a choice. When we allow past experiences and our current circumstances to dictate our beliefs, feelings, thoughts, and actions, we end up being controlled. However, we are in control when we exercise our God-given freedom of choice. Our conscious decisions will then produce results that are in harmony with our desires.

- # -

Thoughts & Inspiration

Personal success is created by first seeking the kingdom of God and then harmonizing with the will of heaven. It is not the struggle to surpass others or surmount difficulties that creates success. It is a willing compliance with the will of God that enables us to produce permanent, positive growth.

Personal wealth and abundance are measures of success, but true and lasting success is contingent upon an ideal higher than the mere accumulation of riches. Earthly possessions, including money, do not fulfill our desire to progress eternally, to become more, and to grow into what we know is our eternal potential.

The genuinely wealthy allow themselves to be a channel through which the infinite God of heaven manifests the miracles of His power and expression. This mindset extends beyond material wealth; it encompasses the rich tapestry of human experiences, relationships, and growth. True prosperity is measured by how much love and service we give.

Service can take many forms. It might be a kind word offered to someone in distress, volunteering at a local charity, or simply being present for those who need support. Each act of kindness creates ripples that contribute to a more prosperous community and abundant world.

By focusing on serving others selflessly, we transcend our limitations and tap into God's infinite source of strength and creativity. This synergy between divine guidance and human action not only fosters individual fulfillment but also contributes to collective well-being, empowering us to make a significant difference in the world.

True wealth comes not from getting more but from contributing more. It is through the act of giving that we realize our true potential and create a lasting impact on the world around us. When we share our knowledge, skills, resources, and time with others, we enrich their lives and our own. This generosity fosters connections and builds communities that thrive on mutual support, bringing us joy and a sense of fulfillment.

The essence of true wealth lies in the quality of relationships we cultivate and the positive change we inspire. By focusing on what we can give rather than get, we shift our perspective from scarcity to abundance. In this way, each contribution becomes a building block for a better future.

Wealth is measured in abundance, but abundance is shallow unless it enables us with a more remarkable ability to give, contribute, serve others, and produce abundance for others. True wealth means becoming more to be able to contribute more. It is not merely about amassing money or possessions but about growing as a person—intellectually, emotionally, and spiritually—so you can make a positive impact on the lives of others. This holistic view of wealth emphasizes that our greatest assets are our abilities to love, give, teach, and empower others, motivating us to commit to our own personal growth.

When we contribute more, we automatically receive more as a direct result. When we consciously interact with God's will, we produce successful results. We are at cause and create effect.

We should not attempt to outline the procedure by which God will manifest our desires. The finite cannot inform the infinite. We are to simply state our desires to God and not counsel Him on how to provide them.

"The superior," wrote Brigham Young, "is not to be directed by the inferior." [104]

True wealth is not the accumulation of money but the ability to be of more remarkable

---

[104] Young, Brigham, *Journal of Discourses* 4:29.

service. It is found in the richness of our relationships, the depth of our experiences, and our positive impact on others' lives. True wealth lies in acts of kindness, moments of joy, and a meaningful connection to those around us. It is reflected in how we use our time, energy, and resources to uplift others and contribute to the betterment of society.

"If, by industrious habits and honorable dealings," wrote Brigham Young, "you obtain thousands or millions, little or much, it is your duty to use all that is put in your possession, as judiciously as you have knowledge, to build the kingdom of God on earth." [105] The more open we are to giving, the more we are open to receiving. This is true of everything. If we want more love, we must first be more loving. If we want more respect, we must first be more respectful. If we want more prosperity, we must first be more giving. We can open up to the channel of receiving by giving more.

---

[105] Ibid.

By now, we should all be familiar with the law of sowing and reaping. The more we sow, the more we reap, and we always reap more than we sow. A single apple seed produces many apples. A single wheat kernel yields almost a hundred new kernels. We are always sowing. To reap what we desire in life, we only need to figure out how to sow those same desires. If we want financial prosperity, we must find a way to help others prosper. The method for achieving anything we want is to help others achieve what they want.

A study has been conducted on lottery winners. Many of those who have won a million dollars or more are farther in debt in five years than before they won. The problem was that they received more, but they never became more. To have more, we must be more. We can be more by being of service in bigger and better ways. Service means being ready, willing, and able to give, contribute, and make a positive difference when called upon.

It is important to remember that it is impossible to be valiant in the cause of Christ when our hearts are set on the ways of the world. We cannot serve two masters and give complete allegiance to either one. But when we seek first the kingdom of God, all these things will be added to us.

Thoughts & Inspiration

SEEK FIRST THE KINGDOM OF GOD

STEPS FOR PUTTING FORMULA

NUMBER SIX INTO EFFECT

I will seek first the kingdom of God in my personal life by committing to do the following:

1. I will seek to know the mind and will of the Lord pertaining to me and my existence. Using my agency, I will strive to act in accordance with His will in all things.

2. I will seek to serve others by sharing the abundant blessings God has given me.

3. I will practice the law of the harvest by sowing the seeds I want to reap.

The Law of Probation

"Purpose is what gives life its meaning."

C. H. Parkhurst

"There is no road to success but through a clear strong purpose."

Munger

The seventh and final Forever Formula for Success is the law of probation. It is having a purpose in our earthly existence. The law of probation states that we have come to this earth to fulfill a specific objective in life.

A principle ingredient of success is having a clear and strong intention and a solid conviction of the value of our mission and purpose. We must first believe in our ability to succeed and then become so completely devoted to it that we make a continuous effort until we reach our goals and aspirations. Success based on weakness and irresolution cannot survive.

The philosophy that we are not human beings having spiritual experiences but are spiritual beings having human experiences is quite common and prevalent. Essentially, we are here to discover our higher, spiritual selves. "This mortal shall put on immortality, and this corruption shall put on incorruption." [106] This is the first requirement and fulfillment of the law of probation. We must discover that we are gods and goddesses in embryo wanting and waiting to be born.

The second component is to find the purpose or mission for our being here. As Alma stated, "Therefore this life became a probationary state; a time to prepare to meet God, a time to prepare for that endless state which has been spoken of by us, which is after the resurrection of the dead." [107]

God's eternal plans and purposes for us are based on the fundamental propositions of joy and happiness. Our divine Father intends for us to find happiness, and our intention should be the same as God's. Unfortunately, happiness is not something that God can simply give to us. As Alexander

---

[106] Mosiah 16:10.
[107] Alma 12:24.

Magoun explains, we must earn it: "Life, the raw materials of this earth, and the timeless unchangeable authority of laws which govern nature and human nature are gifts of God; the rest we must learn and earn for ourselves, including happiness."

Brigham Young has declared that: "It is plainly set forth that there are men preappointed to perform certain works in their lifetime, and bring to pass certain ends and purposes in the economy of heaven... [God] has set up his kingdom among us, and the people had better look to it closely and see that each one is performing his and her duty faithfully. If we do this then all will be well." [108]

Jacob teaches: "Wo unto him... that wastest the days of his probation, for awful is his state." [109] We waste the days of our probation by knowing the law and refusing to obey it.

---

[108] Young, Brigham, *Journal of Discourses* 11:253.
[109] 2 Nephi 9:69.

The third component of the law of probation is to obey the commandments and the word of God as revealed to us. "And we will prove them herewith, to see if they will do all things whatsoever the Lord their God shall command them.

"And they who keep their first estate shall be added upon." [110]

If we cannot free ourselves from the things that draw us and hold us to the world, we are not yet prepared for the new experiences and blessings God is waiting to bestow on us. Abraham's marvelous adventure with Isaac on Mount Moriah would never have taken place if Abraham had not had a great sense of obedience. The young man who came to Jesus to learn what he must do to have eternal life was asked to sell his earthly belongings and give to the poor. His sense of obedience was not nearly so great, and given his goodness in other matters, we can't help

---

[110] Abraham 3:25, 26.

but wonder how great he might have become had he complied. [111]

Take a moment to ask yourself: "What is my purpose in life?" This question is the basis for the development of all philosophies. It is one of the questions behind all religions. Even science, examining the laws governing the universe's unfolding, seeks the answer. "Why do I exist?" is the question of everyone everywhere.

"To be what we are, and to become what we are capable of becoming," wrote Robert Louis Stevenson, "is the only end of life."

Many of us look for the answer outside of ourselves. Not finding it there, we slowly learn to ignore the question altogether. But the answer is easy to see when we look within. We should all realize that we are intimately connected with an omnipotent God and

---

[111] See Matthew 19:16-22.

understand the potential that "the father and I are one."

When we look within, we see the true purpose of our existence. Once we have a purpose, we can find the power to persist until we succeed.

The answer to why we are here becomes apparent when we realize we are individual channels through which Heavenly Father expresses His holy purposes. When God said, "This is my work and my glory, to bring to pass the immortality and eternal life of man," [112] He was also saying that this is *our* work and *our* glory.

Our free agency allows us to choose and enables us to create what we desire. What we create in and of our lives can glorify the Eternal Father. What we create can contribute to bringing to pass the immortality and eternal life of man. We have the power to be a vehicle through which the purposes of God unfold on

---

[112] Moses 1:39.

the earth, and this responsibility is a testament to our agency and potential.

This is the actual business of life. Understanding our purpose, exercising our agency, and aligning our actions with the Divine can lead to a life of fulfillment and service. This is the essence of the law of probation, and it is a guiding principle that can inspire and enlighten us all.

- # -

Thoughts & Inspiration

God acts through His children. We are the channels of His activity. Orson Pratt explains that: "Abraham and many others of the great and noble ones of the family of spirits, were chosen before they were born, for certain purposes, to bring about certain works." [113]

When we begin to understand and accept that our purpose in life is identical to God's purpose, we become motivated to act. We begin to feel God's power in our lives. This motivation fires the imagination, lights the torch of inspiration, and enables us to connect with the infinite powers of heaven. We then become the mechanism through which the Father acts.

---

[113] Pratt, Orson, *Journal of Discourses* 1:58.

Understanding our purpose in life is not just a guiding light, it's a source of empowerment. It shapes our goals, influences our actions, and helps us navigate life's challenges. With a clear sense of purpose, we can align our efforts toward achieving what truly matters to us, ultimately leading to a more satisfying and impactful life.

Understanding our values is crucial in defining this purpose. Self-reflection allows us to discover what brings joy, satisfaction, and a feeling of accomplishment. This awareness empowers us to prioritize activities that resonate with our core beliefs.

Those who recognize their divine purpose and live it become the leaders in our society. If we desire the deepest level of success and life fulfillment, we can achieve it by having a clear and definite purpose, knowing our highest values, and committing to living them daily. "The secret of success is constancy of purpose," wrote Benjamin Disraeli. Aligning our actions with our core values creates a sense of harmony and integrity in everything we do.

This alignment acts as a guiding light that informs our decisions, shapes our priorities, and drives us forward even when faced with challenges or obstacles. Living purposefully means being intentional about how we spend our time, energy, and resources; it calls for setting meaningful goals that resonate deeply with who we are at the core.

It is essential to cultivate self-awareness and continuously reflect on whether we are staying true to ourselves and growing along our chosen path. Self-reflection provides valuable insights into what works well and where adjustments may be necessary. It empowers us to make conscious choices rather than simply reacting to circumstances.

People today often need a clear vision or idea of their purpose or what is most important to them. They evade issues rather than confronting them. The world to them is gray, and they rarely take a stand for anything or anyone. "A person with a half-volition," stated Thomas Carlyle, "goes backward and forward, and makes no way on the smoothest road; but the person with a whole volition advances on the roughest, and will reach his purpose if there be even a little wisdom in it."

When we are unclear about what is important to us, we cannot expect to lay the foundation for a truly successful existence. "The person without a purpose," continues Carlyle, "is like a ship without a rudder. Have a purpose in life and, having it, throw such strength of mind and muscle into your work as God has given you."

When we gain a clear understanding of our purpose in life, making decisions becomes simple. With clarity comes confidence, and with confidence, every step we take is imbued with a sense of direction. Obstacles may still arise, but they are no longer insurmountable; instead, they become challenges that fuel our growth and strengthen our resolve.

Knowing our purpose threads meaning through each moment in the grand tapestry of life. It acts as a beacon during difficult times and as a magnifier during moments of joy. When decisions are aligned with this deeper understanding, an intrinsic peace accompanies even the most arduous choices.

The irresistible force of our ultimate purpose controls the direction of our lives. Purpose leads us to make decisions that create our life direction and ultimate destination.

"In the morning, fix thy good purposes; and at night examine thyself what thou hast done, how thou hast behaved thyself in word, deed and thought," states Thomas Kempis.

In a 1954 conference talk, Richard L. Evans stated, "There is much loneliness in life—not only the loneliness that comes from lack of companionship with people—but also the loneliness that comes from lack of purpose."

A purposeless life is lonely and frightening. People who have found the will to achieve can face the fiercest battles of life. Without that sense of purpose, people become overwhelmed with helplessness and despair.

The pursuit of purpose fosters resilience. Each setback is viewed not as a defeat but as an opportunity for deeper insight and self-improvement. This perspective cultivates perseverance, a quality essential for navigating life's unpredictability.

Ultimately, living with purpose infuses every action with significance. As we move forward on this purposeful path, we inspire those around us to seek their own unique calling. Thus, a ripple effect of intentionality and fulfillment begins, spreading through families, communities, and the world.

- # -

Thoughts & Inspiration

Now is the time to step up and take charge of our actions. It's a decisive moment when we realize our 'response-ability', our ability to respond to the world around us. We become 'response-able' when we are 'able' to 'respond.' This is not a burden but a source of empowerment and control over our lives.

We have now learned that we are at cause. We have learned that to create more for ourselves, we must create more for others. Now is the day of our probation, when we are to fulfill our divine destiny. It is a beautiful destiny of light, love, and abundance. To participate, we must be willing to become all we can become. This is not a time to make excuses. It is now time to be proactive, make choices, and make a contribution.

Seize opportunities with both hands and take deliberate steps towards your goals. Each decision you make, however small, can propel you forward. By fully engaging in your endeavors and embracing the power of initiative, you'll shape your destiny and positively impact those around you. Your active participation is essential; don't wait for change to come—be the catalyst that creates it.

We can claim the gift of purpose and utilize the force that shapes our destiny when we make certain that we have a clear purpose in life—a real and honest meaning for our existence. "No wind blows in favor of a ship with no port of destination," wrote Michael de Montaigne. This journey of self-discovery and growth is what will lead us to our true purpose.

William James wrote, "Compared with what we ought to be, we are only half awake. Our fires are damped; our drafts are checked. We are making use of only a small part of our possible mental and physical resources… The human individual thus lives usually far within his limits: he possesses powers of various sorts which he habitually fails to use. He energizes below his maximum, and he behaves below his optimum."

When we worry about our future success, we are worrying on the wrong end of the scale. We need to look closer at the other end and concern ourselves with finding and fulfilling our unique purpose. To achieve this, we must engage in deep self-reflection and exploration. Understanding our passions, strengths, and values is crucial in uncovering what truly drives us. Once we have a clearer sense of our purpose, it becomes easier to set meaningful goals that align with our inner motivations.

It is essential to recognize that fulfilling our purpose often involves overcoming challenges and stepping out of our comfort zones. Growth occurs when we push ourselves beyond familiar boundaries and embrace new opportunities for learning and development. We can be great right where we are, and our success will take care of itself.

"You may inquire whether we believe in foreordination," wrote Brigham Young, "we do, as strongly as any people in the world… We also are free to choose or refuse the principles of eternal life. God had decreed and foreordained many things that have come to pass, and he will continue to do so; but when he decrees great blessings upon a nation or upon an individual, they are decreed upon certain conditions." [114]

The pursuit of purpose is an ongoing process rather than a final destination. As we evolve over time, so too may our understanding of what gives our lives meaning. Remaining open to change and committed to continuous self-reflection allows us to adapt and refine how we express our unique essence in the world.

---

[114] Young, Brigham, *Journal of Discourses* 10:324.

Thoughts & Inspiration

THE LAW OF PROBATION

STEPS FOR PUTTING FORMULA

NUMBER SEVEN INTO EFFECT

I will put the law of probation into effect in my personal life by committing to take the following steps:

1. I will recognize that I have godly powers and attributes and will work at developing the highest in me.

2. Through obedience, prayer, and inspiration, I will align my earthly purposes with God's purposes for His children.

3. I will learn and obey the commandments of God.

No Secrets

"There are no secrets of success. Success is doing the things you know you should do."

Wilford A. Peterson

"If we live our religion, we shall prosper."

Brigham Young

Success is a lifetime's work built on perseverance, dedication, and the continuous quest for improvement. It involves setting goals, overcoming obstacles, and learning from both failures and triumphs along the way. Each step contributes to a more extensive journey where resilience, a source of immense power, becomes just as important as ambition.

Accomplishments or milestones don't necessarily measure true success; it's also defined by profound character development, relationships nurtured, and the positive impact one has on others. It's about finding fulfillment in everyday efforts and celebrating small victories that pave the path to more remarkable achievements.

As we navigate life's challenges—be they personal or professional—the knowledge gained from our experiences shapes who we are and how we approach each new opportunity. In essence, success is not an endpoint but an ongoing process of growth and exploration; it requires adaptability in an ever-changing world.

Achieving genuine success means committing to lifelong learning while staying true to our values, cultivating passion, nurturing connections with others, and maintaining gratitude for every experience encountered along this remarkable journey called life.

The more we become, the more we are capable of becoming. Our potential is infinite and limitless. We have the power to create anything we desire in our lives. "When we center our lives on correct principles," wrote Stephen R. Covey in his book Principle-Centered Leadership, "we become more balanced, unified, organized, anchored and rooted. We have a foundation for all activities, relationships, and decisions. We also have a sense of stewardship about everything in our lives, including time, talent, money, possessions, relationships, our families, and our bodies. We recognize the need to use them for good purposes and, as a steward, to be accountable for their use." [115]

The only limitations to achieving our maximum potential are the arbitrary and self-imposed beliefs that we can relinquish and replace with more outstanding, empowering beliefs. By disciplining ourselves to become proficient at the Forever Formula, we can reshape our reality through a simple, conscious decision to take control and utilize proven techniques.

We understand now that our method of thinking controls the circumstances and experiences of our lives.

---

[115] Covey, Stephen R., *Principle Centered Leadership*, p. 22.

Given this awareness, we must recognize the power of our thoughts and beliefs. By consciously directing our mental energy towards positive and constructive ideas, we can shape our reality in a way that aligns with our true desires and aspirations. This principle highlights the importance of mindfulness, self-awareness, and intentional thinking in creating a fulfilling life.

It is essential to cultivate an inner environment where empowering thoughts can flourish. This involves regularly monitoring and adjusting our thought patterns, challenging any negative or limiting beliefs that may arise, and replacing them with affirmations that support growth, success, and well-being.

Taking control of our thought processes entails being proactive about the information we consume and the influences we allow into our lives. Surrounding ourselves with uplifting people, engaging in activities that inspire us, and continuously seeking knowledge that enriches our minds are all crucial steps toward fostering a mindset conducive to personal development.

As we begin to master the art of deliberate thinking—aligning it consistently with intention—we'll notice profound changes not only within ourselves but also in how external events unfold around us. Our experiences mirror what we've nurtured inside—joy or discordance, opportunities or obstacles, love or indifference.

We understand now that we choose every thought and that our thoughts shape our destiny.

With this understanding, it becomes imperative to cultivate a mindset filled with positivity, purpose, and deliberate intent. By consciously directing our mental energy towards empowering beliefs and constructive ideas, we set the stage for a future brimming with opportunities and growth.

It is equally crucial to be mindful of the influences surrounding us, as they can significantly impact our thinking patterns.

Surrounding ourselves with supportive individuals, enriching environments, and uplifting experiences can reinforce our positive outlook and help us stay aligned with our goals.

Moreover, practicing mindfulness techniques such as pondering or journaling can enhance our self-awareness and enable us to recognize when we are straying from productive thoughts. This awareness allows us to recalibrate quickly, ensuring we remain on a path consistent with our aspirations.

Mastering the art of intentional thinking empowers us to navigate life's challenges and harness them as stepping stones toward realizing our highest potential. Nurturing a disciplined mind focused on growth-oriented thoughts makes each day an opportunity to create a better version of ourselves and thus craft a fulfilling narrative for the chapters ahead in the journey of life.

We now understand how to increase the power of our thoughts by attaching love and desire to them.

To truly harness this power, we must consistently focus our intentions. Doing so aligns our thoughts with our deepest values and aspirations, creating a more profound impact on ourselves and the world around us. This process involves three key steps:

1. **Clarity:** Clearly define what you desire or love. Vague goals lead to vague results. Be specific about your intentions.

2. **Emotion:** Attach strong positive emotions to your thoughts—joy, excitement, love, passion—all act as powerful catalysts that propel your ideas into action.

3. **Consistency:** Regularly revisit your goals and passions through pondering, visualization, or affirmations; consistency strengthens the neural pathways associated with those desires.

We understand now how to believe in the objects of our desire.

This belief acts as a catalyst, igniting our passion and motivating us toward action. It's not merely a passive wish; it requires commitment and persistence. Each day presents an opportunity to reaffirm this belief by taking small steps toward making those desires a reality.

Through visualization and positive affirmations, we create mental imagery that aligns with our goals. This practice helps us foster an emotional connection to what we seek, reinforcing our determination even when obstacles arise. Surrounding ourselves with like-minded individuals with similar aspirations further amplifies this effect; their support can propel us forward.

Embracing setbacks as learning experiences rather than failures cultivates resilience. As we navigate challenges on the path toward achieving our desires, we evolve, gaining strength and wisdom from each encounter.

Believing in the objects of our desire transforms them from mere fantasies into attainable milestones along life's journey. We become active participants in shaping our destinies instead of passive dreamers waiting for circumstances to change around us. The power lies within—we must harness it fully to manifest what we truly want.

We have no excuses for not succeeding.

We can choose to be more.
We can choose to do more.
We can choose to have more.

By first putting what we want to create into life, we will get out of life precisely what we wish.

We become more by contributing more. We become more by offering more of ourselves. We become more by reprogramming the limiting thoughts running through our subconscious minds. We become more by exercising our free agency. We become more by choosing more. When we choose more, we can then accomplish and do more. When we accomplish more, we attain more. We can have more if we are always willing to give more.

George Q. Cannon said, "We are very progressive in theory, but our theories are far ahead of our practice." [116] We can change this by daily focusing on what we desire. We need to affirm the reality of what we want in life. We must concentrate our efforts on what we want to become. We should demand much more from life.

People often decide what they want by describing what they do not want. We cannot, however, describe light by talking about darkness. Likewise, we should not explain what we want by focusing on what we don't want. We will not achieve peace by denouncing war. We can, however, achieve peace by becoming peaceful. We will not find love simply because

---

[116] Cannon, George Q., *Journal of Discourses* 13:96.

we despise hate. We find love by spreading love. We will never attain great wealth through hating poverty. We attain wealth by becoming abundant. We will never achieve anything by affirming its opposite. However, we will achieve the focus of our thoughts and desires, whether negative or positive.

We will always create our reality by conscious intention. Our thoughts, beliefs, and actions shape the world around us. Each decision we make sends ripples through the fabric of our lives, influencing our personal experiences and impacting those we interact with.

By harnessing the power of the Forever Formula, we can align our intentions with our desires. This alignment allows us to manifest outcomes that resonate deeply with who we are as children of God. The process involves recognizing limiting beliefs that may hold us back and replacing them with empowering ones that support growth and fulfillment.

We cultivate a mindset centered on possibility rather than limitation and open ourselves to new opportunities and pathways. Visualizing the life we want becomes essential, and we actively take steps toward it, trusting that each small action contributes to a larger transformation.

In doing so, we're not merely passive observers in life; instead, we're active participants shaping our destiny. Embracing this responsibility invites an exhilarating sense of freedom and accountability for what unfolds in our existence.

We can shape our reality by affirming the potential existence of the new life we desire until we actually believe in it. Then, we must idealize (not idolize) that desire and expect its manifestation. If we can express gratitude in advance for what we desire, it will show up.

Sterling W. Sill has advised us, "When we live by the principles of success, we cannot be defeated or discouraged." We must plant the seed and then expect the fruit. Know that it will come to pass because that is the basis of faith. It is the natural flow from the unseen to the seen. [117]

We live in a truly remarkable world. People all over the world are awakening to a knowledge of the truth. As they come to an understanding of the "things which have been prepared for them," they, too, realize that, for them personally, "eye hath not seen, nor ear heard, neither hath it entered into the heart of man" the magnificent splendor which exists for those who find the promised blessings. All they ever willed, wished for or dreamed about is but a faint concept of the dazzling reality awaiting them. [118]

Truth is the product of a developed consciousness. The level of truth we can comprehend and incorporate into our thoughts and actions determines our lives, actions, and personal influence in the world.

---

[117] See Hebrews 11:1.
[118] See 1 Corinthians 2:9.

Truth does not manifest itself in creeds but in character.

If our words are harmonious, we will create pleasant conditions. If our words are discordant, we will create uncomfortable situations. If our thoughts are in harmony with what we want, we will find harmony in our lives. Our outer world will reflect the inharmonious condition of our inner world, but by cultivating positive thoughts, we can transform our reality.

"Success or failure," counseled David O. Mackay, "is determined by your ideals, by what you think about when you do not have to think."

We can consciously direct the success of our lives instead of being passive recipients of its activity. The mind pervades every part of the physical body. The body can receive direction from and be impressed by the authority of the objective and dominant position of our minds. What we are today is the result of our past thinking and we shall become tomorrow what we think about today.

Nothing that can be thought of is impossible. As Napoleon Hill suggests: "That which the mind can conceive and believe, it can achieve." Our thoughts definitely direct and create our reality.

God is the great choreographer of all that takes place in billions of galaxies throughout the universe, with elegant, exact precision and unfaltering intelligence. His intelligence is ultimate and supreme, permeating every fiber of existence.

"And the light which shineth, which giveth you light, is through him who enlighteneth your eyes, which is the same light that quickeneth your understanding.

"Which light proceedeth forth from the presence of God to fill the immensity of space—

"The light which is in all things, which giveth life to all things, which is the law by which all things are governed, even the power of God who sitteth upon his throne, who is in the bosom of eternity, who is in the midst of all things." [119]

Every living creature is an expression of God's intelligence. This same supreme intelligence has created and given us the formula that determines our eternal success. This Forever Formula for Success is a potent pool of principles that enable us to attain self-mastery.

When we focus on this formula for lifelong achievement and timeless success and practice the steps outlined in this book, we will recognize that we can create the physical manifestation of anything we desire that is for our good—all the affluence, money, and success we want. We will also recognize that

---

[119] D&C 88:11-13.

our lives will become more joyful and abundant. This Forever Formula for everlasting success comprises the spiritual laws of life that make living worthwhile.

"Principles apply at all times and in all places," taught Stephen R. Covey. "They surface in the form of values, ideas, norms, and teachings that uplift, fulfill, empower, and inspire people. The lesson of history is that to the degree people and civilizations have operated in harmony with correct principles, they have prospered." [120]

---

[120] Covey, Stephen R., *Principle Centered Leadership*, p. 19.

"But it is written, Eye hath not seen, nor ear heard, neither have entered into the heart of man, the things which God hath prepared for them that love him." [121]

---

[121] 1 Corinthians 2:9.

THOUGHTS & INSPIRATION

The Forever Formula

In a Nutshell

DIVINE POTENTIALITY AND INHERITANCE

1. As a child of God, I will develop my relationship with my Father in heaven by actively listening to the voice of His Spirit.

2. I will control my mental attitude and practice thinking positive, uplifting, and pure thoughts. I will keep my thoughts focused on the conditions I wish to create in my life and not allow them to wander in aimless streams of semi-consciousness.

3. I will find the time and make the effort to pray effectively for at least 15 minutes each day.

CONSECRATION AND SACRIFICE

1. I will unselfishly give something to everyone I meet, even if it is only a smile, a compliment, a prayer, a positive thought, or a desire. As long as I am giving, I will be receiving.

2. I will be open to receiving. I will, with gratitude, receive all the gifts life has to offer me in whatever form they may come.

3. I will commit all that I am and all that I have, my wealth, my property, my time, and my talents, to building God's kingdom on earth.

THE VIRTUE OF OBEDIENCE

1. I will become consciously aware of the choices I make daily.

2. I will ask myself two questions before every choice I make;
   a. What are the consequences of the choice I am making?
   b. Will this choice bring success and happiness to me and those around me?

3. I will be in tune with the Light of Truth and seek guidance in making choices through the Spirit of Christ. When a choice feels comfortable, I will proceed. I will pause and seek a more precise answer when a choice raises doubts and discomfort.

1. I will learn to love myself. As I come to love myself, my love for others will increase. I will not think that I am better than other people. I will have patience with their faults.

2. I will learn to love my neighbor. When I feel uncharitable toward anyone, I will pray to have those feelings removed.

3. I will study the life of Jesus Christ, learn what He did in certain situations, and then do the same things when I am in similar situations. The better I know God, the more disposed I will be to look with compassion on others.

1. I will clearly define my goals using specific and measurable terms. I will write down each goal along with a plan for its achievement and commit to reviewing my list daily, thereby staying committed and focused on my journey.

2. Through faith, I will become conscious of my inner power and draw on that power by conceptualizing and visualizing what I desire, thereby feeling inspired and motivated by the empowerment it brings.

3. I will express gratitude for what I do not yet have but am working to accomplish. This could be through daily prayer, affirmations, writing in a gratitude journal, or simply acknowledging the progress I've made toward my goals.

1. I will seek to know the mind and will of the Lord pertaining to me and my existence. Using my agency, I will strive to act in accordance with His will in all things.

2. I will seek to serve others by sharing the abundant blessings God has given me.

3. I will practice the law of the harvest by sowing the seeds I want to reap.

1. I will recognize that I have godly powers and attributes and will work at developing the highest in me.

2. Through obedience, prayer, and inspiration, I will align my earthly purposes with God's purposes for His children.

3. I will learn and obey the commandments of God.

Success Quotes

"If you want to fly, give up everything that weighs you down."

"Setting goals is the first step in turning the invisible into the visible."
Tony Robbins

"Be humble. You could be wrong."

"A dream written down with a date becomes a goal. A goal broken down into steps becomes a plan. A plan backed by action becomes reality."

"Every one of us aspires to a more Christ-like life than we often succeed in living. If we admit that honestly and are trying to improve, we're not hypocrites—we're human.
Jeffery R. Holland

"You can, you should, and if you're brave enough to start, you will."
Stephen King

"Stop focusing on how stressed you are and remember how blessed you are."

"Trying to be happy by accumulating possessions is like trying to satisfy hunger by taping sandwiches all over your body."
George Carlin

"Education isn't something you can finish."
Isaac Asimov

"Men and women who turn their lives over to God will discover that He can make a lot more out of their lives than they can. He will deepen their joys, expand their vision, quicken their minds, strengthen their muscles, lift their spirits, multiply their blessings, increase their opportunities, comfort their souls, raise up friends, and pour out peace."
Ezra Taft Benson

"What fascinates me is that hardly anyone is wondering what we're actually doing on this planet. Most accepted the work-eat-entertainment-sleep cycle as life and have no desire for a deeper understanding of our purpose in this universe."
Jim Carrey

"The highest reward for a man's toil is not what he gets for it but what he becomes by it."
John Ruskin

"It takes as much stress to be a success as it does to be a failure."
Emilio James Trujillo

"Dare to live the life you have dreamed for yourself. Go forward and make your dreams come true."
Ralph Waldo Emerson

"A person is limited only by the thoughts that he chooses."
James Allen

"If serving is beneath you, then leadership is beyond you."

"CTRL + ALT + DEL
Control yourself.
Alter your thinking.
Delete negativity."

"The best way to gain wisdom is by applying God's word to your life."

"Our life is what our thoughts make it. A man will find that as he alters his thoughts toward things and other people, things and other people will alter toward him."
James Allen

"Seek His will in all you do, and He will show you which path to take."
Proverbs 3:6

"Power is not revealed by striking hard or often, but by striking true."
Honore de Balzac

"I am always doing that which I cannot do, in order that I may learn how to do it."
Pablo Picasso

"The reward of a thing well done is to have done it."
Ralph Waldo Emerson

"Spectacular achievement is always preceded by unspectacular preparation."
Robert H. Schuller

"Definitiveness of purpose is the starting point of all achievement."
W. Clement Stone

"The greatest error of a man is to think that he is weak by nature, evil by nature. Every man is divine and strong in his real nature. What are weak and evil are his habits, his desires and thoughts, but not himself."
Sri Ramana Maharshi

"I find the great thing in this world is not so much where we stand, as in what direction we are moving—we must sail sometimes with the wind and sometimes against it—but we must sail, and not drift, nor lie at anchor."
Oliver Wendell Holmes, Jr.

"We are wiser than we know."
Ralph Waldo Emerson

"If you realized how powerful your thoughts are, you would never think a negative thought."
Dr. Caroline Leaf

"Perseverance alone does not assure success. No amount of stalking will lead to game in a field that has none."
I Ching

"There is only one success—to be able to spend your life in your own way."
Christopher Darlington Morley

"A man must be big enough to admit his mistakes, smart enough to profit from them, and strong enough to correct them."
John C. Maxwell

"For myself I am an optimist—it does not seem to be much use being anything else."
Sir Winston Churchill

"You are always one decision away from a totally different life."

"The only safe place for a sheep is by the side of his shepherd, because the devil does not fear sheep; he just fears the shepherd."
A. W. Tozer

"Experience is not what happens to you, it is what you do with what happens to you."
Aldous Huxley

"If you know you can do better, then do better."

"Sometimes you have to play for a long time to be able to play like yourself."
Miles Davis, Jr.

"Small opportunities are often the beginning of great enterprises."
Demosthenes

"Self-assurance is two-thirds of success."
Gaelic Proverb

"Failure is instructive. The person who really thinks learns quite as much from his failures as from his successes."
John Dewey

"Nothing great was ever achieved without enthusiasm."
Ralph Waldo Emerson

"Everyone should learn to do one thing supremely well because he likes it, and one thing supremely well because he detests it."
Brigham Young

"The first and greatest victory is to conquer yourself; to be conquered by yourself is of all things most shameful and vile."
Plato

"Your limits are defined by the agreement you've made about what's possible. Change that agreement and you can dissolve all limits."
Dr. Wayne Dyer

"Success is never a straight line."

"You can do very little with faith, but you can do nothing without it."
Samuel Butler

"When you follow your bliss… doors will open where you would not have thought there would be doors; and where there wouldn't be a door for anyone else."
Joseph Campbell

"The man without a purpose is like a ship without a rudder—a waif, a nothing, a no man. Have a purpose in life and having it, throw such strength of mind and muscle into your work as God has given you."
Thomas Carlyle

"A wise person watches his words; a conscious person watches even his thoughts."

"In the world of business, the people who are most successful are those who are doing what they love."

"You must master a new way of thinking before you can master a new way of being."

"The cave you fear to enter holds the treasure you seek."
Joseph Campbell

"The secret to change is to focus all your energy not on fighting the old but on building the new."
Socrates

"The person who makes a success of living is the one who sees his goal steadily and aims for it unswervingly."
Cecil B. Demille

"The great test of life is to see whether we will harken to and obey God's commands in the midst of the storms of life. It is not to endure storms, but to choose the right while they rage."
Henry B. Eyring

"In reading the lives of great men, I found that the first victory they won was over themselves… Self- discipline with all of them came first."
Harry S. Truman

"If you want to be successful in this world, you have to follow your passion, not a paycheck."
Jen Welter

"The man who acquires the ability to take full possession of his own mind may take possession of anything else to which he is justly entitled."
Andrew Carnegie

"With self-discipline most anything is possible."
Theodore Roosevelt

"The bravest are surely those who have the clearest vision of what is before them, glory and danger alike, and yet notwithstanding go out to meet it."
Thucydides

"Don't pray when it rains if you don't pray when the sun shines."
Satchel Paige

"You always miss 100% of the shots you don't take."
Wayne Gretzky

"Nothing is a waste of time if you use the experience wisely."
Auguste Rodin

"What lies behind us and what lies before us are tiny matters compared to what lies within us."
Ralph Waldo Emerson

"A creative man is motivated by the desire to achieve, not by the desire to beat others."
Ayn Rand

"Know from whence you came. If you know whence you came, there are absolutely no limitations to where you can go."
James Baldwin

"The spirit, the will to win, and the will to excel are the things that endure. These qualities are so much more important than the events that occur."
Vince Lombardi

"No one ever gets far unless he accomplishes the impossible at least once a day."
L. Ron Hubbard

"Success is how high you bounce when you hit bottom."
George Smith Patton, Jr.

"The strongest factor for success is self-esteem; believing you can do it, believing you deserve it, believing you will get it."

"Successful men and women keep moving. They make mistakes, but they don't quit."
Conrad Hilton

"Success is not what you have, but who you are."
Bo Bennett

"There is no disinfectant like success."
Daniel J. Boorstin

"Happiness lies in the joy of achievement and the thrill of creative effort."
Franklin D. Roosevelt

"Without continual growth and progress, such words as improvement, achievement, and success have no meaning."
Benjamin Franklin

"Success does not consist in never making mistakes but in never making the same one a second time."
George Bernard Shaw

"We often discover what will do, by finding out what will not do; and probably he who never made a mistake never made a discovery."
Samuel Smiles

"To do good things in the world, first you must know who you are and what gives meaning to your life."
Robert Browning

"During my 87 years I have witnessed a whole succession of technological revolutions. But none of them has done away with the need for character in the individual or the ability to think."
Bernard Mannes Baruch

"If a man will begin with certainties, he shall end in doubts; but if he will be content to begin with doubts, he shall end in certainties."
Sir Francis Bacon

"Success is no accident. It is hard work, perseverance, learning, studying, sacrifice, and most of all, love of what you are doing."
Pele

"The indispensable first step to getting the things you want out of life is this: decide what you want."
Ben Stein

"Success is where preparation and opportunity meet."
Bobby Unser

"Success usually comes to those who are too busy to be looking for it."
Henry David Thoreau

"There are no limits to what you can accomplish, except the limits you place on your own thinking."
Brian Tracy

"If the plan doesn't work, change the plan, not the goal."

"If you have no critics, you'll likely have no success."
Malcolm X

"Consistency is the key to success."

"A positive attitude will lead to positive outcomes."

"Focus on the possibilities for success, not the potential for failure."
Napoleon Hill

"There are no secrets to success. It is the result of preparation, hard work, and learning from failure."

"If you don't sacrifice for what you want, what you want becomes the sacrifice."

"The key to success is action, and the essential in action is perseverance."
Sun Yat-sen

"Focused, hard work is the real key to success."

"Clear your mind of can't."
Solon

"I try to do the right thing at the right time. They may just be little things, but usually they make the difference between winning and losing."
Kareem Abdul-Jabbar

"Never esteem anything as of advantage to you that will make you break your word or lose your self-respect."
Henry Brooks Adams

"If you're not failing every now and again, it's a sign that you're not doing anything very innovative."
Woody Allen

"We are what we repeatedly do, excellence is therefore not an act but a habit."
Aristotle

"Belief in oneself is one of the most important bricks in building any successful venture."
Lydia Maria Francis Child

"Success in life is a matter not so much of talent as of concentration and perseverance."
C. W. Wendte

"Success is not the key to happiness. Happiness is the key to success."

"The path to success is to take massive, determined action."
Tony Robbins

"Try not to become a man of success, but rather try to become a man of value."
Albert Einstein

"Success consists of going from failure to failure without loss of enthusiasm."
Winston Churchill

"It takes twenty years to build a reputation and five minutes to ruin it. If you think about that, you'll do things differently."
Warren Buffett

"A strong, positive self-image is the best possible preparation for success."
Dr. Joyce Brothers

"Your positive action combined with positive thinking results in success."
Shiv Khera

"The most successful people are those who take pride in their work, pride in their family. It is great to attain wealth, but money is just one way—and hardly the best way—to keep score."
Kemmons Wilson

"The most successful people do not make up rules as they go. They have a set of rules that they follow, and they stick to them."
John Chancellor

"Success in business is passion combined with fearless execution. The most successful people I know focus on the things they can control and perfect the details."
Gina Bianchini

"Successful people are not gifted; they just work hard, then succeed on purpose."
G. K. Nelson

"Successful people are usually just regular people who are doing the things that most people are afraid to do."

"The most successful people are those who are good at Plan B."
James A. Yorke

"The most successful people are the ones that work on themselves first."

"Success does not lie in results but in efforts. Being the best is not so important, doing the best is all that matters."

"Successful people are simply those with successful habits."
Brian Tracy

"Act as if what you do makes a difference. It does."
William James

"Readiness for failure is a prerequisite for success. Even the most successful people fail. Strong people become stronger."

"Successful people make the most of the best and the best of the worst."
Steve Keating

"It is literally true that you can succeed best and quickest by helping others to succeed."
Napoleon Hill

"The most successful people, the evidence shows, often aren't directly pursuing conventional notions of success. They are working hard and persisting through difficulties because of their internal desire to control their lives, learn about their world, and accomplish something that endures."
Daniel H. Pink

"The greatest danger for most of us is not that our aim is too high and we miss it, but that it is too low and we reach it."
Michelangelo

"Successful people are always looking for opportunities to help others. Unsuccessful people are always asking, what's in it for me?"
Brian Tracy

I hope you have enjoyed reading this book and that it brings you closer to achieving true success in your life.

I would love it if you could post an honest 5-star review on a book site where you have an account and posting privileges. Maybe you can mention what you liked best about this book or how it helped you in some way.

I hope that you will tell your friends about this book if you find it enjoyable, educational, or inspirational.

About the Author

Stephen R. Gorton is an award-winning poet and published author of dozens of books, articles, and blogs.

He has also worked in the Healthcare and Mental Healthcare Industries and as a Personal Financial Consultant.

Contact Stephen at:

stephen@greenstemmedia.com

9 798227 759054